D1648267

BE STRONG!

The Making of a Marked Man

Be Strong!

What Others are Saying about *Marked Men for Christ* and the book, *Be Strong*...

The witness of a Christian man shows in the way he lives his life, out loud and with purpose; by the way he loves his wife and his family; and by the way he boldly proclaims his faith in Jesus Christ. Steve "Spice" Spicer exhibits all of these. Saint Augustine says it well: "Every sinner has a past, and every saint has a future." You must read Spice's story of knowing his sin, his brokenness, and his journey toward holiness.

> **--Rev. John Lager**, OFM Cap and Cofounder *Marked Men for Christ* ministry

I have been blessed to walk alongside my husband, Steve "Spice" Spicer, throughout the journey of *Marked Men for Christ*. He is a courageous, faithful leader who surrenders himself to Jesus every day to lead MMFC. With the encouragement of my husband and the other cofounder of *Marked Men for Christ* (John), Women's Walk With Christ (WWWC) ministry was also created. As the Executive Director of WWWC, I have been privileged to witness Jesus' work through the power of the Holy Spirit to heal and transform the lives of men and women through these two ministries. Our marriage is continuously strengthened as well. Lives have been changed, marriages have been saved, and so much more!

> **--Debi Spicer**, Wife and Executive Director, Women's Walk With Christ ministry

I wouldn't be where I am today without my Pops, Steve Spicer. I have learned countless things from him in many different aspects of life. His love, wisdom, and strong leadership portrayed what it takes to be a man. As he continues to lead men with MMFC, it is nothing short of life-changing.

> **--Zach Spicer,** *Marked Man for Christ*

I experienced a profound transformation through the Phase One experience of *Marked Men for Christ* in April 2017. I began to see my wounds as they were and anticipate their healing by the Lord Jesus Christ throughout the process of my sanctification. I recommend enthusiastically MMFC ministry to all men that are struggling with their remaining sins and crippling wounds.

>--**Dr. Sung Wook Chung,** Professor of Christian Theology at Denver Seminary, Littleton, Colorado; President of Kurios International, a global missional organization

I was hesitant to add yet another men's event to my life for the first few years I heard about *Marked Men for Christ*. However, after my mom died after a sudden diagnosis of cancer, I struggled to cope with grief in a healthy way. I was hiding from several important relationships in my life. I attended Marked Men Phase One event just a few months after her death, and I realized the freedom that Christ can give me when I am aware of my brokenness and my gifts at the same time, and as I turn both over to Him. This life-changing ministry has given me the tools to dive deeper in relationships with my family and friends, and I have learned to allow others to connect on a more relational level with me.

>--**David Childs,** Chief Listener & President of Spartan Planning Group, and Global Director *Marked Men for Christ* ministry

Ten years ago, my husband and I were in dire straits with our 23-year marriage. Despite counseling, it wasn't until he spent 44 hours on a *Marked Men for Christ* weekend that our marriage began to heal and transform. When he returned home on Sunday evening, it was evident that a complete miracle had happened. His heart of stone had become a heart of flesh.

>--**Rhonda Whyte**, wife of a *Marked Man for Christ*

God's grace, love, and mercy poured over me at my Phase One weekend in September 2010. The Spirit of God set me free from the shackles of doubt, fear, and depression. His love melted my self-imposed anger and helped me discover a brotherhood of men

Be Strong!

devoted to living in The Light and out of the shadows of deceit and darkness. I am honored to share the message and ministry of what God is doing through *Marked Men for Christ* around the globe. By God's grace, Steve Spicer's story has now been replicated in over 10,000 men.

> **--Jim Phillips**, *Marked Men for Christ*, Director for Africa

I know of no other ministry that gets into the heart of a man more effectively than *Marked Men for Christ*. I am tremendously grateful that MMFC gave me deep healing, and the ministry continues to help me move out of my head and into my heart. I recommend this to every man who desires to follow Christ with more passion and purpose.

> **--William Bolthouse** MD and Global Director *Marked Men for Christ* (MMFC) ministry

Through *Marked Men for Christ*, Jesus has captured my heart in a unique way that is masculine though gentle, providing a clear vision of my life´s mission. God sowed a hunger for Scripture and expanded my heart for Christians all over the world, no matter their church background. Praise to JESUS for what he has done in my life through *Marked Men for Christ*!

> **--Markus Mayr**, *Marked Men for Christ*, Director for Europe

When I first came to the MMFC weekend, I had already been in ministry for twenty years and I had an MA degree in theology, so I thought nothing could surprise me. That weekend changed my mind. I dared to go deep into the furthest corners of my heart which I had always tried to avoid. That was just the beginning of a great work which God continues to produce in my life.

> **--Hennadiy Nebeskul,** Pastor at Island Christian Church, Ukraine

Marked Men for Christ is a ministry God has raised up for such a time as this. It is a fulfillment of Ezekiel 37, where God is pouring out His Spirit on dried up, defeated men to become a mighty army for His glorious grace. It is a fulfillment of Isaiah 61 where Jesus is healing brokenhearted men and setting them free to find His joy as their strength. I have watched men restored to the joy of their salvation, and they are excited again to be servants of Jesus' church and kingdom.

> --**Pastor Clyde Godwin,** Director of The Barnabas Center Triad and Global Director *Marked Men for Christ* ministry

I attended my first *Marked Men for Christ* Phase One weekend in January 2010. Simply put, I found amazing healing from a lifetime of anger. The ongoing Phase 3 (small group) I attend gives me a place to grow stronger and go deeper with Christ and my brothers. God has called me to help men find their place on the battlefield, and MMFC is a great vehicle for me to accomplish this.

> --**Lee Paige,** retired airline pilot; Director for *Priority One Ministry*; SE Region Director for MMFC

I accepted Jesus at age 47. After three years of discipleship training, a friend invited me to a *Marked Men for Christ* Phase One experience. I learned to embrace Christ's freedom by cutting loose all of my old baggage, and my life has been transformed!

> --**J. Marc Williams,** Retired U.S. Army Colonel

As a pastor, I first approached *Marked Men for Christ* with an academic attitude – "what can I learn to help others?" What I found was a blessing for myself. Shortly thereafter, I called the Academic Dean of my former Bible College and noted that if I were in his role, I'd require every male student to participate in an initial MMFC Phase One weekend before graduating. Many ministries for men promise change; MMFC delivers.

> --**Steve Hinton** – Pastor, Author of *Confessions: Finding Hope Through One Pastor's Doubt*

It's more powerful than any conference, meeting, revival or service I've attended in 34 years of active ministry. The *Marked*

Be Strong!

Men for Christ 44-hour intense experience is one of four major life-changing experiences I've had. It shaped me in ways I never imagined possible. The other three are my initial commitment to Jesus, my marriage to the most incredible woman on earth, and my getting deeply involved in overseas missions in Africa, all of which continue to shape and sharpen who I am today and who I will be tomorrow and beyond.

> **--Joe Agro,** Retired Youth Pastor; Director, *Adopt One Village Hunterdon,* President and Managing Member, *AutoDrill,* LLC

I have been a Christian for 47 years and involved with men that entire time. When I was introduced to MMFC 6 years ago, I thought it would be just another good men's group...until I went to the Phase One weekend and was astounded at the vulnerability and change in men's lives (and my own). There is nothing like it!

> **--Steve Kurtz,** Vice President of Mortgage Finance at Corporate Investors, Global Director *Marked Men for Christ* ministry

Marked Men for Christ has been a catalyst for me to be bold in my faith, to gain clarity in my Godly mission — what God calls me to do and be, and to live and work intentionally in my life roles. I am a better man, husband, father, grandfather, leader, coach, servant. My life has greater meaning, purpose, and fulfillment. I am a stronger man for Jesus Christ and with Jesus Christ.

> **--Ray Reuter,** President Kaizen and Senior Co-leader of *Marked Men for Christ*

Having staffed 57 Phase One weekends, I have seen many healings and miracles! I remember one deeply troubled younger man from Colorado who stood on the bank of a river, yelling "FREEDOM." Another was a 70-year-old man from North Carolina who finally was able to forgive his deceased dad after 60 years of living with anger!

> **--Mel Claytor,** mentor for Spice; formerly on Board of Directors for *Marked Men for Christ* ministry

The Phase One Weekend Experience and the ongoing support of my Marked Men Brothers have helped me grow in my relationship with Jesus. [These have] given me tools to weather the challenges and hardships of life. Praise God!!!

> **--Greg Ham,** entrepreneur and Global Director *Marked Men for Christ* ministry

I thank God every day for MMFC. Before Greg went to his Phase One weekend in January 2013, our marriage of 28 years was heading towards a divorce. Today, my girls and I are proud of the husband, father and man he's grown to be. I'm also grateful for our counselor that loved Greg enough to invite him to such a life-changing weekend. Thank you, Michael, and *Marked Men for Christ* (MMFC) for giving me my husband back.

> **--Tressa Trahan**, wife of a *Marked Man for Christ*

In January 2013, I was invited to a MMFC Phase One weekend in the mountains of Colorado. Although on the OUTSIDE it seemed I had the world and life going my way, on the INSIDE I lived such a huge lie and carried so much shame and brokenness daily. This weekend without a doubt was life changing, not only for me personally, but my wife and girls are so thankful for the husband and dad they have today. I'm grateful, humbled, and blessed to have had someone love me enough to invite me to such a powerful weekend. Praise God!!!

> **--Greg Trahan**, entrepreneur and Global Director *Marked Men for Christ*

Marked Men for Christ is a healing and transformational experience. *Marked Men for Christ* principles in practice has helped me to become happier and loving. I am blessed!"

> **--Denis Hoelting**, original member of Board of Directors for *Marked Men for Christ*

"God has transformed my life, ministry and marriage in a radical way through *Marked Men for Christ*. I now live a new life in mission, serving my family, church and the world, because of the healing Jesus has done in my life thru this ministry."

--**Pastor Randy Stensgard**, Plymouth Covenant Church

Through *Marked Men for Christ*, God brought to my life the truth that I needed. Now I am a man who lives out his life with passion and mission for Christ. Be Strong!

--**Pastor Hector Luis Rosario**, Dominican Republic

Marked Men for Christ is not a one-time event, but rather a transformational experience. It is a way of life where I am loved, accepted, and strengthened by my Christian brothers in the pursuit to be a stronger man for Jesus Christ for my wife, my son, and all people God places in my path. I believe *Marked Men for Christ* is a movement that is impacting God's kingdom in all the corners of this world.

--**Michael "Bear" Abare,** MMFC Heartland Regional Director

My dad is a loving father. He started *Marked Men for Christ,* and I am blessed to be part of it. I have served on over fifty Phase One weekends in three countries. I love it!

--**Scott Spicer**, Marked Men for Christ

As the wife of a *Marked Man for Christ*, I can say with great joy that this ministry is foundational to our marriage. My husband has staffed at more than twenty weekend experiences, and here's what I know: nothing presses the reset button on his heart like serving alongside these men. When Peter serves in the healing work, our entire family wins.

--**Tricia Lott Williford,** author, speaker, teacher, and wife of a *Marked Man for Christ*

BE STRONG!

The Making of a Marked Man

Steve "Spice" Spicer

with T. L. Heyer

FaithHappenings Publishers
Centennial, Colorado

Be Strong!

Unless otherwise marked, all Scripture quotations are from the NIV, Zondervan Corp (a division of HarperCollins Publishers), all rights reserved

FaithHappenings Publishers
A division of WordServe Literary
7500 E. Arapahoe Rd., Suite 285
Centennial, CO 80112
303.471.6675

Cover Design: Dionisio C. Manalo Jr.

Book Design: Greg Johnson

Interior Illustrations: Alex Kraft

Ordering Information:

Quantity sales. Special discounts are available on quantity purchases by corporations, associations, and others. For details, contact the "Special Sales Department" at the address above.

Steve Spicer, Oct 2, 1959

First Edition

ISBN: 978-1-941555-42-2

To...
My high school sweetheart
My Wife
My Love

Debi

Be Strong!

Table of Contents

Chapter One: Start Here 19
Wounds are Real
Chapter Two: Deceit 23
What Mask Do You Wear?
Chapter Three: Fear. 37
What Are You Afraid Of?
Chapter Four: Anger 51
"Get Out of My Way"
Chapter Five: Sadness 65
Grieving the Losses of Hopes, Dreams, Relationships
Chapter Six: Shame 77
Not Good Enough
Chapter Seven: Forgiveness .93
Giving and Receiving Forgiveness
Chapter Eight: You are a Holy Man 103
How to Walk in Holiness
Chapter Nine: Mission and Life Purpose 113
What Is My Life All About?
Chapter Ten: Conclusion, Commission 129
Invitation to *Marked Men for Christ*

Devotions: 21 Days for the Making of a
Marked Man for Christ 139

Be Strong!

Healing is born from other people's testimonies. In this book, you'll find a lot of my story, my personal testimony, and how I have sought healing from my pain and anger. My desire is to show you the fruit God has brought to my life, and the fruit He can bring to yours. Testimonies from my life and the lives of other men can paint that picture, but it is God who does the healing.

I have prayed over this book as I've written it, and I am praying for you as you read it. My prayer is that you will feel inspired to be MORE like JESUS. I hope you begin to feel an awareness of your weakness, for that awareness creates space for His healing strength in your life.

Let's move, men. BE STRONG!

Steve "Spice" Spicer
April 2019

Acknowledgements

I'd like to thank my brothers, Gary Beckie and John Lager, for caring enough to have coffee and heart-to-heart discussions with me in 1999!

I'm also thankful for the 11,000$^+$ brothers-in-Christ who encourage, inspire and model their hearts' desire to GROW STRONGER in their faith!

"Be on your guard; stand firm in the
faith; be courageous; be strong."
1 Corinthians 16:13

Chapter One
Start Here

Wounds are Real

Let's begin with the stories of some men I know, men of character and strength, men who are perhaps a lot like you and me.

Terry is a leader in his church and community, a family man raising two daughters with his wife of two decades. He's your go-to guy if you need someone to lead. He knows the Bible well, he's great in front of a crowd, he is confident in his circles of friends. Nobody would guess that Terry's addiction to pornography has a hold on him. And he has told himself it's the least dangerous of all the possible addictions, because he's not really hurting anyone. Sure, he's not proud of it. In fact, he's very ashamed of this pattern. And he knows as a pastor and leader, the very last thing he can do is tell anyone, or all of his valued and respected roles will diminish in a heartbeat.

James is a very successful businessman. Or, rather, James *was* a very successful businessman. He was on a path to early retirement from this company he started from the ground up, until his business partner made some decisions that benefited only himself. He took advantage of James' trust, his friendship, and his financial status, and James got screwed in the deal. He is seething with anger...absolutely boiling with rage over the ways he was irrevocably wronged. James has no idea how to move forward, and he doesn't really want to. To move forward would imply that it was okay, what happened to him. So he's carrying explosive rage with him, all directed toward this former business partner, but now bleeding into all of his other relationships.

Dan never felt like he was good enough for his dad. As the second born son in his family, there was never anything novel about him. He felt like a perpetual disappointment—not a born athlete, not a born leader, not a born academic, and not even the firstborn, a most coveted mantle in his family. Dan has always felt like he wasn't enough, didn't have enough, didn't bring enough, didn't know enough, couldn't be enough.

Isaac's marriage is in trouble, circling the drain in a long, slow downward spiral. Isaac's wife has asked him to join her for marriage counseling, but that seems beside the point now. This can hardly be fixed, this friendless marriage of two adults who barely know one another anymore. He's not sure what went wrong, or where they went wrong. His parents' marriage was always his model, and he treated his wife and his kids the same way his dad had treated his own family: with authority. Isaac has never told anyone that he was molested when he was eight years old, a secret carried by his father's brother, the uncle who molested him. It's a dark truth he has carried close, never spoken aloud, because how could he begin to say those words, and who would have believed him? This awareness of the secrets people keep has manifested into a controlling nature, so he keeps a tight rein on his wife and children at all times. If he can keep them under control, then he can keep them safe, he tells himself. Isaac's fear has grown into a monstrous need to be in charge and in control, and he has become the bully of his own family.

I'll always remember my second trip back to Kenya with *Marked Men for Christ*. A staff man approached me with great joy and shared, "Spice, I am so grateful for *Marked Men for Christ ministry!* It has changed my life!"

"Really? What changed?" I asked him

He said, "I realized that I needed to start loving my wife like Jesus instructed us in the Bible. So, I stopped beating her, and I started encouraging her. My marriage is much stronger!"

"Well done, pastor!" I replied.

You see, these men carry wounds. Perhaps you carry wounds as well.

Perhaps you are carrying a burden of anger that is not serving you well. Maybe you are paralyzed by shame over something you have done, or maybe something done to you. Perhaps fear is controlling you, and you go about your days with a mental checklist of all that you must protect, defend, and control. Or perhaps you are experiencing sadness over a loss—the loss of a relationship, a dream, an innocence. The nature of wounds is that they cannot heal themselves, and the longer they go untended, the more they fester and spread into otherwise healthy places of our lives. These wounds can keep you from becoming the man you long to be, the man God created you to be.

Men, you are NOT alone. Thousands of men before you have struggled with these very same situations, and they have become stronger men in Christ through the healing of their wounds. I promise you this: God wants to heal you and move you forward to a place of abundance and wholeness. The first step of healing is the awareness that one is broken. This is where radical life change begins.

Are you ready?

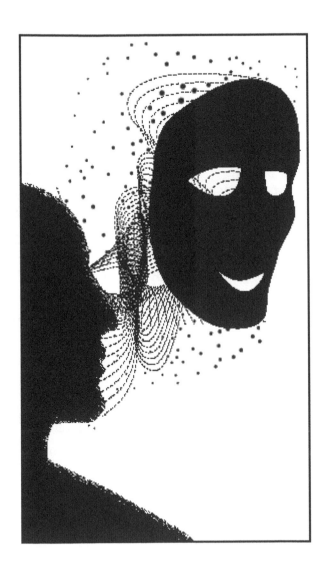

Chapter Two
Deceit

"What Mask Do You Wear?"

My First Masks

I have a long history of wanting to fit in. This wound goes back a long way. As a child, I was always the biggest kid in my class. In fact, in first grade, I was almost twice the size of the other first graders. By the time I was in fifth grade, I was wearing Husky blue jeans, the Sears brand of pants for big and chubby kids. To my great mortification, the word *Husky* was printed on the back of the pants for all the world to see. I remedied this by tying a windbreaker around my waist, all hours of the day. Keep in mind: we lived in Fort Lauderdale, Florida. It was hot. There was no air conditioning. I hardly needed a jacket on hand to keep a chill away, but I wore that windbreaker around my waist every day, so you couldn't see that I had Husky pants on. I covered it up.

When I was in sixth grade, my family moved from South Florida to Central Texas. What a culture shift that was! We moved to a different state with a very different vibe, and we bought a ranch. The nearest town was seven miles away, and our nearest neighbors were a mile away. We lived at the end of an isolated dirt road, the picture of isolation. I wanted so badly to fit into my new world—no longer the Florida kid, but now a Texas rancher.

My parents took us to Mexico the following year, and I got my first pair of cowboy boots. They had an orange tint, and they were significantly less expensive than the boots made in America.

But I noticed that the American-made boots had a sewn-on tip over the toe of the boot. The toe was a different color than the rest of the boot. I didn't have that kind, but I so badly wanted my

> *I was willing to do whatever I needed to do to cover up the person I didn't want to be.*

boots to look like the other boots. So, I took black shoe polish, and I painted a tip on my boots. I'm sure anyone could tell that I had hand-drawn the black toe. There's no way I made it look professional. But I wanted to fit in, and I'd do anything to make it happen. It was my first mask of deceit.

As you can see, I got an early start. Whether I was painting the tips of my boots to fit in or covering up the label of my true and authentic (husky) self, I was willing to do whatever I needed to do to cover up the person I didn't want to be.

The Football Scene

I started playing football when I was in eighth grade and let me tell you this: there is no bigger sport than football in Texas. Stadiums are built in small towns, exclusively for the local football team. Football is king, and I truly found myself on that football field, in many ways. I progressed on the team, and I moved up to varsity football as a freshman.

I earned a scholarship to Rice University in Houston, Texas, where the average SAT score was in the top percentile. The school was packed with smart kids. Of the ninety guys on our NCAA Division I football team, we were all the best in our graduating class from high school. I had been the top athlete of my senior year, but on the college scene, I was just one of many top athletes from many high schools. They were better than me. Stronger, faster, and quicker. How would I get to play? How would I stand out? The first thing I needed to do was to find a way to fit in. I started doing everything they were doing – only bigger or better. If they had a bong in their room, I got a bong for my room. If they were smoking dope, I'd smoke it better. If they were drinking, I'd drink more. I learned to take everything to the next level. I'd do anything to fit in with my peers, to stand out.

What did I get from fitting in and standing out? Acceptance. I wanted those guys to like me and love me. So, I became Mr. Entertainment. That's the mask I wore. We would go to bars where the loudest table would win free beer. College scholarship athletes aren't allowed to have a job, so we couldn't earn any money to pay for our partying. But I assure you, we could be loud. There was a *lot* of free beer for the loudest table. I remember vomiting all over the table, only to empty my stomach and keep on drinking. It didn't matter to me. I just wanted them to see how funny I was, how much fun I was, crazy enough to make myself sick in public. I sent a clear message: you want to have a good time? Invite me to your event. If you want to get crazy, I'll get crazy with you.

My teammates and I were deeply into excessive partying, and we learned we were above the law. You see, not only were we students at Rice University, an elite school of high pedigree, but we were NCAA *football players*. If we were ever pulled over by the city police, we knew to present not only a driver's license, but also our Rice University Student ID. With that combination, the police would typically let us go. No arrests, no ticket, no problem. We were special. Those were our masks, and nobody could touch us behind them.

In my junior year of college, our team flew on a chartered flight to Lubbock, Texas to play Texas Tech University. On the flight, we had the dignitaries of the Rice University, the entire coaching staff, and the traveling team. After our game, I snuck a six-pack of beer on the plane, ignoring a very important rule: alcohol was prohibited for any athletes at any NCAA event. We were covering up the sound, drinking them behind our seats, feeling invincible. Stupidly, we left the cans on the plane behind us. We thought the flight attendants would simply assume it was left over from another flight, so it was no big deal. But we failed to consider that our chartered flight had no other passengers. They saw our six empty cans, and they reported it to the coaching staff.

We flew into Houston late on Saturday night, and we had a team meeting on Sunday morning. All ninety players were there, and our head coach stepped up to the podium. "We've got a problem on the team,"

> *At that point in my life, I knew the church, but I didn't know Jesus.*

he said. "Someone on this team is breaking NCAA regulations." He held up one of the empty Coors cans. The crowd went dead quiet.

"We know it happened on that flight. There were no beer cans before you got on, but there were empty cans when you got off. One or more of you drank on that plane. There will be consequences for breaking the NCAA rules as well as our own team rules against alcohol consumption during a football event. We're going to ask who in this room drank out of this can, and that person will be punished. Be a man. Stand up and own it."

I was guilty. Not only had I drunk, but I had been the one to bring the beer on the plane. But I chose to hide behind my mask. I pretended I was innocent. I did not stand up. Nobody stood up.

So, the coach said, "All right, we'll do this one more time. If nobody stands up to claim this, then the entire team will be punished. This team will run until one of you confesses."

Nobody stood up. Several teammates and I were hiding behind masks, claiming to be innocent when we were clearly guilty. And so, we ran. The whole team ran and ran and ran. We ran on Sunday, we ran on Monday, we ran on Tuesday, and we ran on Wednesday. Nobody ever confessed.

Now, on one hand, I can tell you that we were an exemplary definition of a team. We were all in it together. In one way, that's a powerful definition. But you can flip that around and say it's an ugly definition; we all denied the truth together.

Jesus said the truth will set you free[1], but at that moment, a confession didn't feel like freedom. At that point in my life, I knew the church, but I didn't know Jesus. I didn't find Him as my personal Lord and Savior until later that same year, at the end of my junior-year football season in college. But at that point, I didn't know who He was, and I didn't act like a follower of Christ. My relationship with Christ was like that of a small boy.

The Good News and the Truth

Let me tell you the good news of that story. At the end of that football season, one of the football players invited me to an evangelical meeting. This new ministry in town had come to clean up our city of Houston in the name of Jesus. I had grown up Roman Catholic, and evangelicals were completely unknown to me. I walked into that room, and I knew immediately that I had never been in a room like this.

First of all, it was a mixed group of young men and women, but there was no alcohol, no drugs, no partying and no sex.

---

[1] John 8:32

Nobody was taking it to the next level. There was hugging and talking, embracing one another without any of the other elements of parties I knew. Also, they were talking about Jesus stuff. That got my attention. I mean, I knew church, but I didn't know Jesus. My understanding of church was a list of duties and responsibilities. You go every weekend, stand when they tell you, sit when they tell you, and don't talk during the service. But in each of these meetings, these people talked about a relationship with the Savior of the world. That was foreign to my brain.

The guys who had invited me were my teammates. We spent all of our time together—in classes, at practices, in tutoring sessions, three meals a day, and during free time on our own. We had done life together. I trusted these guys. They came back to my dorm room one night, and they said, "Spice, what do you think about these meetings?"

I told them I was intrigued. I had never seen anything like this before—a community like this, a church like this, a Jesus like this. What was this new experience?

They said, "You could have that same personal relationship with Jesus, Spice. Do you want that?"

I did. Very much.

They shared with me Romans 10:9-10 (ESV). "because, if you confess with your mouth that Jesus is Lord and believe in your heart that God raised him from the dead, you will be saved. For with the heart one believes and is justified, and with the mouth one confesses and is saved."

Confession meant something different in my Catholic background. So, I asked them, "How do I confess?"

They said, "Spice, do you believe that Jesus Christ is your Lord and Savior?"

"Yes."

"Then you just confessed that with your mouth. Now, do you believe that in your heart? Do you believe that He died for your sins, that He rose from the grave three days later? Do you believe that deep in your heart?"

"Yes, I do."

"Then you are saved for eternity right now, brother. With your confession and your belief, you are justified in the eyes of God. He sees you as pure, holy, and sanctified, without stain or blemish." My life changed in that moment. Not only my life, but my eternity.

> *"Close your eyes, Spice. Let the Spirit wash over you." And as the Spirit washed over me, a foreign language started coming out of my mouth."*

And then they said something more. They told me, "Spice, God has spiritual blessings for you. Heavenly blessings. You can receive these gifts." I knew nothing about the Bible, so this was all news to me. They began listing for me the gifts God offers to those who call on his name: prophesy, serving, teaching, encouraging, and leading.[2] They explained the blessings that could be mine through the Spirit: miraculous powers, wisdom, knowledge, and speaking in tongues.[3] They talked about the fruits I could bear by the power of the Holy Spirit: love, joy, peace, patience, kindness, goodness, faithfulness, gentleness, and self-control.[4] They explained gifts, callings, and anointings.

I wanted these things. I wanted to be equipped.

---

[2] Romans 12: 6-8
[3] 1 Corinthians 12:7-11
[4] Galatians 5:22-23

They said, "Close your eyes, Spice. Let the Spirit wash over you." And as the Spirit washed over me, a foreign language started coming out of my mouth. I felt like my whole body was elevated out of the chair! It was beautiful and transformational in ways that are difficult to explain. My life was changed forever in that moment. I felt so close to Jesus!

Before that night, the bookshelves in my dorm room didn't have a single book on them. There were plenty of empty bottles of tequila and whiskey, evidence of good times. The next day, though, I knew I could no longer live like this. I got rid of the bottles. I got rid of the bong. I stopped smoking dope and drinking alcohol. It was no longer even attractive to me. Everything had changed.

I saw my old high school friends when I was home for Christmas break, and they were very familiar with the old ways of Mr. Entertainment. They were partying like always, and they were ready for me to join them. But that's not who I was anymore. Debi was my girlfriend at the time, and she could see the change in me. We went to the same parties, but I stopped drinking. Nobody could believe the change, but all I could say is that I had found Jesus. I didn't need to get drunk anymore! I wanted to be done drinking in excess, doping, and running around. I was a new Christian. That was a radical life change that took place, just by accepting Christ into my heart.

A New Creation

I went back to school after Christmas break, the second semester of my junior year. I had a full load of difficult classes, but I had a new mentality and a new approach to life. I started reading Scripture. Like a baby, I took small bites. And I began to invite the Lord into the decisions of my college life.

Instead of thinking about how I could cheat and cut corners, I'd pray as I studied. *Lord, as I read these textbooks, what do I need to remember? What do I need to retain to do well on these tests? Help my brain recall.* As I began to pray this way, my grades began to improve.

When the football season began again, instead of thinking about how I could use all my human talent to win the game, I started to invite the Lord into my football strategy. *Lord, help me to be the best I can be on this play. Maybe the guy across from me is a Christian as well, so I pray for him too. Maximize my skills.* As I began to pray that way, my game began to improve.

I was praying for mental sharpness in my studies. I was praying for physical aptitude in my employment as a scholarship student. I was praying for others, which was entirely new to me. Alcohol was less attractive to me. Masks were coming off, and that felt risky to me. I had to face some hard questions. How would this affect my relationship with Debi? Would I still be funny? Would they still like me? Did those things matter to me as much? I was forming a new relationship with Christ. It would be decades before I'd learn how to receive Him as my friend, but He had become my Lord and Savior. And that changed everything!

No More Masks

The truest self I've ever been was when I was a little boy, before I became adulterated by the world. Can you remember when you were unadulterated? When you were just you? Try to remember when you could feel good about yourself, without wearing any masks. You see, as a little boy or girl, you are just you. You only know how to be you. Good or bad, you're just you, and the people around you love you. You don't have to fit in. If you don't like peas, you won't eat your peas. You know you don't like them, and you're not interested in pleasing others by eating your peas. That is pure authenticity.

I am not perfect, and I can sense when I am putting on a mask to fit in. It doesn't feel good. The good news is that I'm aware of it now, and I can question myself and my reason for putting on the mask. The key is to be my true self. When you are your true self, people don't approach you with things you don't like, because they already know you're not interested. How can we pursue an authentic lifestyle like that, where we attract people of the same values? The answer is to hang out with holy people of good character. Jesus never put on a mask; He never hid from who He was, and He never denied who He was. He was always his true, authentic self. You and I are called to be like Him.

As you are reading this, you may be realizing that you do not yet have a relationship with Jesus Christ. If you have not yet made that decision, I invite you to take off the mask and change everything for this lifetime and for eternity. You can do that now! When you accept Jesus as your Lord and Savior, four things happen:[5]

1. We stand firm in Christ. We are all family members, one body with Jesus at the center NOW and FOREVER!

2. We are anointed. God gives us a life mission and a purpose for the breath He has put in our bodies.

3. There is a seal on each of our souls. I'm marked out for life: I am His, and I belong to him. This is true of you as well. Jesus uses the example that He's the Shepherd and we are his flock. There's a mark or a brand (or a seal) on your soul and mine, and He knows us.

---

[5] 2 Corinthians 1:21-22

4. He gives us the deposit of the Holy Spirit. He abides in us. The Holy Spirit makes his home within us, dwelling in us.

With the deposit of the Holy Spirit into our hearts, it changes the inner core of who we are. He is our helper. He helped me to make the transition to become a man of God, and He can do the same for you. I changed from a man of deceit to become an authentic, truthful, transparent witness of His great love.

Take off your mask, brother. Let Jesus heal you and introduce you once again to the man you were made to be.

*   *   *

Lord, I ask forgiveness for the masks I wear.
I want to be holy as you have created me to be, an authentic man of truth.
Please strip away any masks I hide behind.
You want to deal with the real man I am, not the poser.
Interpret my thoughts. Show me when I am being duplicitous.
Give me an awareness of when I am about to speak outside of my authentic self. Put a guard over my mouth to keep me from speaking outside of the truth you have called me to.
Thank you, Jesus! Amen.

*   *   *

"Woe to you, scribes and Pharisees, hypocrites! For you are like whitewashed tombs, which outwardly appear beautiful, but within are full of dead people's bones and uncleanness. So, you also outwardly appear righteous to others, but within you are full of hypocrisy and lawlessness."

Matthew 23:27-28 (ESV)

As obedient children do not conform to the evil desires you had when you lived in ignorance. But just as he who called you is holy, so be holy in all you do; for it is written: "Be holy, because I am holy."

1 Peter 1:14-16

* * *

BE STRONG!

1. To discover your true self, you need to go back to the beginning, when you were a little boy. Can you remember this little guy? Picture him in your mind.
2. Write down three attributes that you had before you were influenced and adulterated by your environment.
3. What would Jesus say to you, that little guy at that young age?
4. How can you walk in that authenticity today, as a man who desires to be more like Jesus?
5. Invite God to give you an awareness of the masks you wear. If you're not sure where your deception lies, ask God to show you.

Spicer

Be Strong!

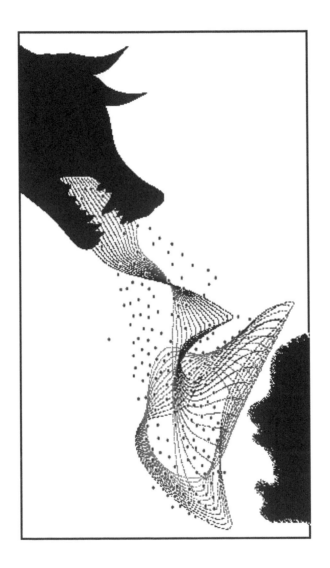

Chapter Three
Fear

"What Are You Afraid Of?"

The Root of Fear

In my earliest childhood experiences, I have no memories of feeling fear. I don't remember being scared. My home was a safe place, I was protected by my parents, and I was unaware of the dangers in the world. I had the nourishment I needed, and all my needs were met. I had a safe and solid start. My first memory of fear emerged in the fifth grade, when I was bullied for the first time.

I mentioned that I was the biggest kid in my class, and my height was especially evident in those years. I was 5'10" in elementary school, so I had to wait a long while for other kids to catch up to my height. In South Florida, we lived in a nice neighborhood, maybe two miles away from my elementary school. I was riding my bike home from school one day when two older kids came up behind me. They grabbed the seat of my bike, and they stopped me in my tracks. They pushed me, threatened me, took my bike, and rode away with it. I was a big kid, but I wasn't a fighter. I had no experience in self-defense. I watched them ride away on my bike, and I gathered myself and walked home, feeling very afraid. It was my first experience with being bullied, my first encounter with fear.

When I got home, my dad was there. He greeted me in the front yard, and I shared with him what had happened. I don't remember exactly his response, but I remember what he did not do: he did not take me down the street to get my bike back. I remember that he stood still, and he did nothing. My protector didn't protect me. I remember my fear taking root in that moment; if my father wouldn't protect me, fight for me, who would?

The middle school years are hard on everybody, and it is an especially difficult time to make a move across the country. When we arrived in our new town in Texas, the bullying continued. I was still the biggest kid, so I was an easy target. Sixth and seventh grade were brutal for me. I had a 45-minute bus ride to and from school, and I was entirely unprotected in that zone of physical and verbal abuse. At the end of the day, I started walking the three miles to my dad's downtown office, and then I'd catch a ride home to the ranch with him at the end of his work day. He probably thought it was some nice father-son time, but I couldn't tell him the truth: I was scared.

The worst bullying happened in the spring of seventh grade. In my junior high school, we ate lunch with our class and then all the grades were mixed together outside for about fifteen minutes before we were called back in for our next class. I remember feeling so alone, walking around and passing the time with no friends, when suddenly a gang encircled me. They pushed me back and forth in their circle, and then they shoved me down to the ground on my hands and knees. In front of all my peers, they mocked me for being so big and so weak. As I knelt on all fours, they forced me to pick up leaves with my mouth. They laughed at me, jeered me, mocked me. In a sea of middle school students, no one helped me. For most of my life, one of my greatest fears was being jumped from behind. I have

> *...do I move toward my fear or not? I need to make a choice.*

no doubt that it stemmed from those two experiences from my childhood, when I didn't see the attack coming.

When I began playing football the following year, I learned for the first time how to use my big body to my advantage. I learned I could use my size as a weapon to move other people, to intimidate them, and even to hurt them if I needed to. I began to carry myself differently. I started lifting weights, shaping my body into something that loomed with intimidation. In fact, I spent a couple of decades lifting weights and especially doing dumbbell curls. I'd warm up with 40-pound weight, and my max would be three sets of three with 100-pound dumbbells. My arms were of a significant size. Big arms look like big threat. I never wanted to feel fear again, so I sent a clear message: don't mess with me.

What Does Fear Feel Like?

Men and women experience fear on a regular basis, a number of times a day. Fear is a stressor, and it brings a physical reaction. I have learned to recognize my bodily sensation to fear, and I know it when I feel it. My fear begins as a knot in my stomach. Then I get chills, and my body actually changes temperature. Then I feel a sensation to choose: do I move toward my fear or not? I need to make a choice.

There are three physical choices in response to fear:

1. Freeze. You can choose to do nothing. Sometimes that's not a good choice. Inaction is an action in itself, and something *will* happen if you do nothing.
2. Run. You can choose to run away from fear. This can be a great choice sometimes, as it can transport you to a place of safety. I personally know someone who was on the 120th floor of the World Trade Center on September 11, and her first response to the attack was to *run*. She did not

wait for authorities to tell her what to do. She ran, and she survived. Others delayed, frozen with fear, waiting for authorities to tell them what to do, and many of those people did not survive. Running can be a strategic move, though not always.

3. See your fear and move through it. You can identify the physical sensation, recognize the fear for what it is, and take steps in the direction of your fear. Again, sometimes this is a great choice, though not always.

So, if we have three clear choices, but none of them are always right, what do we do?

Fear is Real

Fear began in the Garden of Eden, when our great grandfather Adam was afraid. He had sinned, he hid from the Lord, and he said, "I heard the sound of you in the garden, and I was afraid, because I was naked, and I hid myself" (Genesis 3:10 ESV). Fear has been around since the beginning, and there are more than four hundred references to fear in the Bible. Obviously, God knows man, and He knows our weaknesses and brokenness.

We can read Scripture to find multiple examples of God's great men encountering fear. Abraham's fear caused him to make poor and dishonest decisions in two different countries because he was afraid he'd be killed by the men who might want to take his wife.[6] God picked Abraham to serve him, to be the father of many nations, even though Abraham was a scared man.

Elijah the prophet saw God move in amazing ways; he was even a firsthand witness when God sent fire down from heaven. But his flesh was weak, and he knew fear. When Elijah was afraid,

---

[6] Genesis 12:10-13; 12:17-20

he ran for his life![7] Still, we see that God chose Elijah to be his prophet, even though Elijah encountered fear as well.

One of my favorites of God's men is Peter, and he was afraid, too. His name was actually Simon, and he started out as a fisherman. Think about the daily work he did with his hands: he was pulling nets through water, again and again, pulling in fish and algae. That kind of daily resistance training would have given him big arms, shoulders and chest. We can safely imagine he was strong and well-built. On the outside, he even appeared to be a bold leader. In the face of conflict or adventure, he was the first to say, "Let's go." But inwardly, as we learn by his actions, he struggled with fear.

When God met him, He changed his name from Simon to Peter. He replaced the name his parents had given him, and He gave him a new name that means The Rock. Jesus said, "On this rock, I will build my church."[8] He chose him as one of the foundational people to begin His ministry, even though Peter was a man of fear, too. Let's look at an important story of Peter's life, when he was overcome by what he feared.

Three years after Jesus invited Peter to follow Him, they were together at what we now know would be The Last Supper.[9] Jesus turned to Peter and said, "You will all fall away because of me this night." With Peter's great confidence, and maybe you could even call this arrogance, Peter responded with a bold reaction: "Peter said to him, "Even if I must die with you, I will not deny you!" And all the disciples said the same."

---

[7] 1 Kings 19:3
[8] Matthew 16:18
[9] Matthew 26:31-35 (ESV)

But Jesus, knowing Peter, disagreed with him. "Truly I tell you, this very night, before the rooster crows, you will disown me three times."

Then Jesus, knowing where they were headed and what the evening held for them, asked His disciples to get swords to take with them to the Garden of Gethsemane. Now, remember, the disciples were a group consisting of several fishermen, so they had knives with them already. They used them all the time. And just as we might expect, they said, "See, Lord, here are two swords." "That's enough!" he replied." (Luke 22:38)

He took them to the long night in the Garden of Gethsemane. While Jesus went to pray, the disciples kept falling asleep, and Jesus kept waking them. While He was talking to them, the Scripture tells us that the temple guards came to arrest Jesus. In the frantic flurry of activity, one of them struck the servant of the high priest, and some Gospel writers identify Peter as the one who cut off the servant's ear.

> *Peter went from the boldness of fighting an armed man with his fishing knife to then trying to hide in the shadows.*

You see, Peter is a fighter and a warrior. He's the go-to guy. He created this damage with his knife, trying to honor the Lord with his boldness. But then Jesus healed the man's ear, which I imagine is not what Peter had in mind! As the guards took Jesus away, it says in the Bible that Peter followed at a distance. Peter went from the boldness of fighting an armed man with his fishing knife to then trying to hide in the shadows.

The next time we see Peter, he's standing by a fire with townspeople. He's hiding in the shadows of that fire when God sends someone to seek him out. But He doesn't send a giant like Goliath; He sends a woman. Actually, He sends a servant girl. She sees Peter, and she says, "Hey, I know you! You were with him!"

Right then, Peter was faced with a choice: he could be courageous and move through it, he could stand still and do nothing, or he could run. Peter chose to run. Instead of facing the fear and the repercussions of confessing Christ, he denied her claim, saying, "Woman, I don't know him."

But God was not done with him yet. A second time, a woman approached him, and we have to keep in mind that women were not meant to be feared at all. They were considered property in that culture, and they were nothing to be afraid of. But when God sent a second woman to say, "Hey, I know him. He's one of the disciples," Peter *was* afraid. He chose to run again, and he said, "I do not know the man."

I often wonder why God would choose such a weak, fear-filled man to build His church. Why would Jesus choose such a man of weakness? I believe it's because Peter represents most of us men. On the outside, we look like we have it all together. We may lead with a force that looks like courage, just like Peter did. We may even be built big and strong, just like Peter was. But God knows the heart of a man, and on the inside, we are often afraid. I am comforted by the truth of Peter's story: the presence of fear does not mean God cannot use us in powerful, mighty, radical ways.

You see, God had to prove to Peter that he wasn't so tough. He had to reveal to him his own weakness. God tested him one more time, just to show Peter how scared he truly was. This time he sent a man to confront him, and Peter denied Jesus for the third time. In that moment, the rooster crowed. Peter realized what he had done—that he had in fact denied the Messiah,--and the Scripture tells us that he wept.

A Daily Reminder

Have you ever been around a rooster? They start crowing up to 2-hours before the sun rises, and they are faithful to their work as God's alarm clocks to start the day! They're loud and obnoxious. I have to imagine that every day for the rest of Peter's life, he began each morning with the sound of a rooster's crow. Every single morning, the first sound he likely heard was a reminder of the time when he denied Christ.

Peter could have heard that sound and felt rebuked yet again, but that's not what God wants for us. He wants to set us free from our fear, as soon as we recall that our strength comes from Him.

> *Every single morning, the first sound he likely heard was a reminder of the time when he denied Christ.*

I imagine Peter heard the rooster crow, and perhaps he thought to himself, "I will never deny Him that way again. Not today, not ever." And in humility, he started his day with the courage to be fearless, no matter what crossed his path.

You see, we can fast forward into the second chapter of the book of Acts, when the Spirit came upon the early church. Peter was so bold and so courageous, and he preached like nobody ever had. He was a simple fisherman, but Peter preached and taught like someone with a doctorate in theology! He faced threats from the Sanhedrin and the leaders of the Jewish community, but he didn't back down. He was not afraid. He was courageous for Christ because of what Christ had done in him.

The only way we can ever be strong is through Christ. Our strength does not come from our flesh (biceps), but it comes from heaven—from a deposit of the Holy Spirit.

Confess Your Weakness

I mentioned that I lifted weights for a number of years, and I specifically focused on bulking up my arms, all in an effort to make my body bigger and intimidating to any potential threat. In my mid-thirties, this plan started to backfire, as my forearms began to hurt badly. They hurt so badly that I couldn't lift a pen to write.

I went to see a sports medicine specialist, and he asked me to describe my workout. I told him about the dumbbells, the weights, and the daily repetitions. He got a smirk on his face. He said, "Well, Spice, you're breaking down all the small muscles and tendons in your forearms. There are dozens of them, and you're ripping them with this workout you're doing. I see this all the time with weight lifters. I can do surgery to fix this, I can sew all of them back together, but if you keep lifting, you'll tear them again. Eventually I won't be able to repair them, and you won't be able to pick up a coffee cup."

The inability to lift a coffee cup felt like a bleak future.

The doctor told me that I needed to stop lifting heavy weights, and I needed to immediately cut my workout regimen by 50% or more. That felt daunting, though. I'd always lifted weights. It's part of who I am – this build, this shape, these muscles. How could I protect my wife, my children, and myself if I didn't look like an intimidating person who could keep them safe?

> *You don't have to worry that someone will jump you from behind. I've got your back. Trust me.*

I heard from God on that day—and it changed my life! I sensed that He told me, *Spice, you've done a good job of taking care of your body and keeping yourself safe. But now it's time for you to trust* **me**.

You don't have to worry that someone will jump you from behind. I've got your back. Trust me.

There was a gift in the pain. I knew I needed to change the plan, and I got rid of my heavy weights. I still lift at home, but I choose now to work out with light weights, high repetitions, and everything has healed in my forearms. Praise God!

More importantly, my philosophy about fear and protection has changed. Perhaps you can relate to this, men: I used to sit with my back to the wall anytime my wife and I went to a restaurant. I wanted to keep an eye on the door, so I could be ready to protect us against any threat that could enter our space. That feels like wisdom in the moment, but when I dialed it down, I discovered that this decision was motivated by fear. I had modified my behavior in response to my fear, and God asked me to confess that fear to Him, then to trust Him and to believe that He has my back.

> **The only way I can be a courageous man of great faith is to begin by realizing how weak I am.**

Now when I go to a restaurant, I can sit with my back to the door. Not only that, but this courage from the Lord has empowered me to visit places I never thought I'd go to, like East Africa, Ukraine, Russia, and Vietnam. God's got my back! I am safe with Him.

Know Your Source

The only way I can be a courageous man of great faith is to begin by realizing how weak I am. I have to begin with humility, so I do not rely on my own strength and abilities. I can do all things through Christ who strengthens me, and you can as well. But we must never forget the source: *His* strength.

There is no heavenly courage without man first recognizing his own fear. There is no room for God to empower you as long as you believe you can do it on your own. You may feel like you show strength and masculinity when you say you have no fear, but a man with no fear has no need for God! As soon as you confess your fear, your need for God—*Boom!* The confession creates an invitation for the Holy Spirit to come.

You see, it's a beautiful cycle. When we confess our fear, we can receive help. When we receive courage, we can trust. This trust builds our faith, and this faith invites us to confess our fears once more. As I practice this over and over again, I can become a man of deeper and deeper faith. You can experience the presence and strength of the Holy Spirit, every time you confess your fear to Jesus.

*   *   *

Jesus, thank you for making me a man.
I am a man who is afraid, and I confess that fear to you.
As I lay out my fears, I pray that you will replace them with courage.
My courage comes from you, and I can be bold and courageous through you.
As you answer my prayer today, may my faith grow.
I long to be a man of great faith,
living out the Gospel in every aspect of my life. Amen.

*   *   *

"The Spirit you received does not make you slaves, so that you live in fear again; rather, the Spirit you received brought about your adoption to sonship. And by him we cry, "Abba, Father."
Romans 8:15

"The Lord is my light and my salvation—whom shall I fear?

The Lord is the stronghold of my life—of whom shall I be afraid?"
Psalm 27:1

So, we have come to know and to believe the love that God has for us. God is love, and whoever abides in love abides in God, and God abides in him. By this is love perfected with us, so that we may have confidence for the day of judgement, because as he is so also are we in this world. There is no fear in love, but perfect love casts out fear. For fear has to do with punishment, and whoever fears has not been perfect in love.
1 John 4:16-18 (ESV)

* * *

BE STRONG!

1. In Jesus' presence, we can be courageous and bold. How do I find this courage? It starts with recognition that I do have fears. I must begin with the ability and strength to confess this truth.
2. Make a list of some of your greatest fears. List at least five. I'll confess mine to you, in hopes that my vulnerability will guide you to personal truth.
   a. I have a fear of not being good enough.
   b. I fear not having enough money to sustain me to the end of my life.
   c. I fear not having a strong enough body to sprint across the finish line of life. I fear losing control of my body, of lying flat on a bed in a nursing home for the final years or decades of my life.

d. I fear not having the ability to communicate with words, and I fear the inability to see. That would isolate me, and I fear loneliness.

e. I fear not being loved by others. I fear losing my wife to illness or losing my sons to distractions of their lives. I fear being totally alone.

Confess your fears to the Lord. Be honest with God, knowing that your honesty invites the Holy Spirit to enter that space and give you the courage you need. In Jesus' presence, you can be bold.

3. Every morning, Peter heard the rooster crow. That was his daily reminder that he needed Christ to be his strength. We each need Christ every day, so we can be bold and courageous for Him. What is your daily reminder?

a. One idea: Be intentional with the password to your computer, since we each tend to sign on every day. Include the year or your age to represent courage in the present moment. GREATFAITH39. Courage2020. BeCourageous50. This positive affirmation can remind you who you are: a man of great faith, not fear.

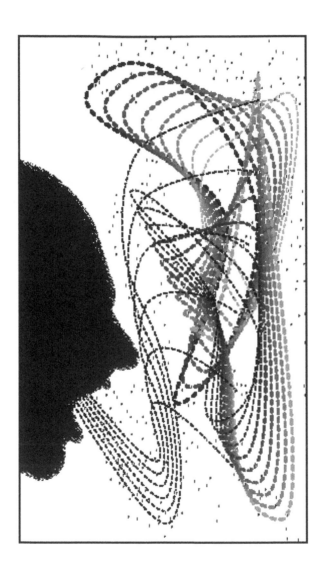

Chapter Four
Anger

"Get Out of My Way"

Anger is not a sin. I want to make sure you hear me say that: Anger is not a sin. How could it be? The perfect man, Jesus Christ, the Lamb of God, was angry. Yet He never sinned.

You remember the Scripture passages, right? You've probably read them, so you remember when Jesus went into the temple, into His Father's house. He walked up to the pigeon seller, and he said, "Excuse me, Mr. Pigeon Seller, but your pigeons are pooping all over my Father's house. Now, I know you have to make a living, and I know your birds are extremely important to you and your family. But they're pooping all over my Father's house. Would you mind moving them out of the way?"

And then Jesus went to the money changer, and He said, "Oh, excuse me, Mr. Moneychanger. I'm sorry to interrupt you. I know that you're charging way too much as you exchange money, but I understand how it is. I know you've got to make a living. If you don't mind, though, this is my Father's house. I hate to ask, but could you move your booth over there, please? I don't mean to disturb you."

Is that the way Scripture reads? Oh, that's not the way you understand it?

Yeah, I don't either.

As a matter of fact, the writer of the book of John, in chapter 2, tells us that when Jesus looked around and saw that they had turned His Father's house into a flea market or a swap meet, the Scripture says that He didn't even go inside immediately. No, with great intention, Jesus made a weapon before He entered that temple. He created a cord of whips to use as He entered His Father's house.

I wasn't there and neither were you, so we don't know exactly how it went down. But Scripture gives us insight, and I can imagine that Jesus, *God Himself*, shouted at them, "Get out! Get out of my Father's house! *Get OUT!*" I imagine that He flipped the tables with His hands, and He kicked them over with His feet, all the while shouting at them. I imagine His voice was loud and guttural, *"Get out!"*

Jesus was angry. Yet He never sinned. His anger was righteous. In fact, Scripture does not tell us that we should never be angry. No, the Bible tells us, "In your anger, do not sin" (Ephesians 4:26a). Jesus was without sin. Scripture allows for anger.

Anger is not a sin.

* * *

One of the big differences between Jesus and me (and there are so many) is that I have definitely sinned in my anger. Far too often, in fact. If you could go back in history to the late 1980s and throughout the 1990s, and if you could look up the definition of Road Rage, you would see a picture of me. Rage is anger that is out of control, and during this time of my life, my anger was absolutely out of control. I was a Road Rager.

You see, I grew up in my father's house, a large property that was both a farm and a ranch. I was the only son, and when you live on a ranch with a lot of work to be done, the son becomes the key source of that labor. My dad loved me, no doubt. But he loved me by giving me food and shelter, by teaching me how to manage money, and by instilling a positive mental attitude and the value of hard work. He didn't give me what my heart needed most: to be loved for just being me, not for what I could produce. My heart yearned to hear from my dad, "Steve, I love you." It was so hard, that I would have to ask my mother if dad was proud of me. The times I heard words of affirmation or love was when I worked hard on the ranch or when I exceeded his expectations in my athletics.

> *Anger is not a sin. How could it be? The perfect man, Jesus Christ, the Lamb of God, was angry. Yet He never sinned.*

Sports became a big part of my life, and the coaches of my Texas football team became my father figures too. In football, I learned that the harder I could hit other players, the more I could please my coach. That's how I could earn my words of affirmation, so I got very good at earning them. I did it so well that I got a four-year scholarship to play Division I football.

Now, if you met me, you'd probably take one look at me and think, "A football player? You're not that big. What were you, an outside linebacker or a defensive end?" No, I was an offensive lineman. And so, you might think, "Wow. He's kind of small to play that position." And you're right. (By the way, I knew that before you did.)

In college, I'd get up to the line of scrimmage, I'd look around and see how much bigger, stronger, and faster my opponent was, and I would feel nothing but fear. But I desperately wanted that affirmation from my offensive line coach. I quickly learned the only way I could take these guys down, the only way to please my coach: I slipped into a crazed state of mind.

Be Strong!

As I would approach that line of scrimmage, I'd look around and take my blocking assignment. I'd look at my opponent, a guy much bigger than me, and I'd access a boiling rage that ran deep within me. I knew the snap count, and I would wait to hear, "Hut! Hut!" In that split second, I would explode off that line. I'd go *crazy*. For those 3-5 seconds during that play, I had just one thought in my head: punish the other guy.

Then, with the opponent successfully blocked, I'd look to the sidelines to see my coach. If I had done my job, he would leap into the air and throw his fist into the sky. I'd hear him shout my name, "Atta' boy, Spice! Atta' boy! Do it again, Spice!"

Every time I saw my coach give me that affirmation from the sideline, it went straight to my heart. I'd go back to the huddle, I'd receive the play, I'd get the snap count. I'd come back to the line of scrimmage, and I'd do it again. I'd do whatever it took to get that affirmation, whatever it took to "beat the other guy."

I played in every game for four years, and I got an NCAA letter for three out of the four years in college. My senior year, I tried out for the Dallas Cowboys, but that was a whole different league. When they finished the tryout, it was very clear that I was too slow, too small, and not strong enough, so I decided to go and get a real job. I married Debi and we moved to New Orleans, where I became a salesman with Procter & Gamble. When I took that new job, they gave me a company weapon.

Oh—wait. Sorry. I meant to say that they gave me a company *car*.

Maybe you've been to New Orleans, and perhaps you've seen the traffic there. They've got a lot of water and a lot of bridges, and that makes for a lot of traffic. It was my job to make eleven sales calls per day, but I learned quickly the secret to real success. See, my boss was another father image, and I was still so hungry to receive love affirmations from a father figure. So instead of making eleven sales calls, I set out to meet or exceed the expectations of my boss, just like I had learned to do on the ranch with my father and on the football field with my coaches. Exceed the expectations, find love.

"Atta' boy, Spice! Proud that you're on our team, Spice! So glad you're on the job today!" I wanted those words every day.

So, around 3:00 in the afternoon, if I only had nine or ten sales calls, I'd start working even faster. I had to get to twelve, thirteen, or fourteen calls a day so I could get that dose of affirmation. I didn't have time for another car or driver to get in the way of the love I needed to hear. If you were driving in front of me in the middle of the afternoon on Interstate 10, I'd pull my company car right up behind you, and first I'd flash my headlights. If you didn't get over when I flashed my headlights, then I'd lay on the horn. And while I was laying on the horn and flashing my lights, I'd watch for your eyeballs to look up into your rearview mirror. And when you looked at me, you'd see me shouting at you, "Get over! *Get over!*"

And you'd best get over.

If you didn't get over, oh, I had a plan for drivers like you. I'd drive my car up alongside yours at the first chance I got. I'd take my company weapon, and I'd jerk my steering wheel to the right, forcing you and your car off the road. Once I got you to the side of the interstate, I'd angle my car right in front of your car so you'd have nowhere to go. I'd trap you in your car. And then I'd get out of mine. I'd walk back to have a word with you. It didn't matter to me how big you are, how tough you are, or even if you're packing heat. You and I were about to have a little conversation, right there on the side of this interstate. It would be time for you to learn a lesson, time for me to teach you how to drive on my streets. You would learn to get out of my way when you're driving in front of me.

Oh, one more thing that I didn't tell you: this road rage was how I operated during the week, Monday through Friday. On Saturday and Sunday, though, I was at your church. Hands up, praising God. Taking communion with you. My wife and I led a couples' Bible study at our house each weekend, because we were "great Christians," and because it was so important to me to teach men how to become better husbands and fathers. You see, I was a leader in your community on Saturday and Sunday.

But Monday through Friday, you better get out of my way.

It worked for me. It worked quite nicely.

I got promoted multiple times in New Orleans, and they eventually gave me a big management job in Dallas, Texas. On a Saturday morning in Dallas, my wife said to me, "Honey, I want to go to the flea market."

I didn't want to go to the flea market. I had my own plans. But I knew that if I wanted to get my love affirmation on Saturday night – men, you know what I'm talking about – then we needed to get in the car and drive to Canton, Texas. *So, let's go then,* I thought. *Right now. Let's go. I have other things to do with my day, so let's get this over with.*

I was heading up the ramp to get onto Interstate 20, and I saw a yield sign. Perhaps they meant for the drivers in my lane to yield as they merged into traffic, but that's not how I operated. I demanded that all other cars would yield to me. And, can you believe it, there was a car on the interstate *not yielding to me.*

So, I sped up. And the car sped up.

I went as fast as I could to get around him. He did the same thing, pacing right beside me.

I finally had no choice but to take my foot off the accelerator, and there's nothing—*nothing*—I hated more.

I was cooking inside. Boiling.

First chance I got, I got right behind him. I started flashing my lights. Laying on the horn. Yelling, "Get over! *Get over!*"

But he didn't get over.

So, I took my car, and I drove right alongside his car. I saw him right beside me, watching me. I was about to teach this guy a lesson.

Now, remember, my wife was sitting beside me, and apparently, she had never seen me do this before. She's maybe all of 5'2" and a half. My wife was trying to tell me something, but I couldn't hear her. I was looking right at that driver, yelling, "Get over! *Get over!*"

I jerked the steering wheel, making this guy pull over. Again, my wife was trying to tell me something, but I couldn't hear her. I had one mission: get that guy off the road.

I ran him off the road, and I pulled my car right in front of us, trapping him in. He had nowhere to go. He was mine now. My wife was still saying something, but I couldn't hear her. I reached down to grab the door handle so I could head back there and have a word with this guy.

As I reached for the door handle, I felt this compression in my chest. *Huh. That's different*, I thought.

I looked down. There was a fist in my chest. And that fist was connected to an arm. That arm was connected to my wife. I looked over at her, into the eyes of my bride. She had been crying for a while, and the tears poured down her face. Her face was pure white, panicked. She had lost her voice from screaming, "Stop! Stop! *Stop!*"

I hadn't heard her at all. My rage was so out of control that only her fist in my chest had gotten my attention.

Suddenly and finally, I heard my wife.

* * *

Now let's jump ahead to August 1999, in a booth at Einstein's Bagels. Two of my best friends had cornered me, and they said, "Spice, this anger you have, this road rage? It's going to kill you. Either you're going to die or you're going to kill somebody else, and you'll be in jail for the rest of your life, separated from your family and everything you love. You need to get some healing."

They had checked out a weekend experience for me, and they wanted me to go.

"Now, Spice, it's not Christian," they said, and then added facetiously, "and we know what 'a good Christian guy' you are. Before you say no, we're going to tell you that we have a plan. We're going to bring Jesus with us. We will go with you, and we will pray with you as they set up a safe experience for you to get that anger out of your heart."

I was nervous.

But I trusted these men. I knew they loved me.

On a Saturday afternoon, they set up this anger experience. The first time they set it up, I sliced through it like a hot knife through butter. I was so frustrated that it didn't give me the healing I needed. I was ready to abandon it all and go home, back to my patterns and my rage.

But I praise God for a guy named John Lager, my good friend and brother, and now my cofounder for *Marked Men for Christ* ministry. He wouldn't let me go. John grabbed me by my shirt, and he got in my face. He said, "Don't you leave! Don't you quit! You trust God! Trust me! Don't you quit!"

And so we ran it again. This time, with lots of prayer, I went through that exercise differently. I realized on that day that I was filled with raging, unresolved anger toward my father. He didn't give me what my heart needed, which was simply love for being his son. I just wanted his love, not

> *"Don't you leave! Don't you quit! You trust God! Trust me! Don't you quit!"*

a reward for what I could produce or do for him. I was able to release my anger in a safe place and in a safe way, where nobody got hurt. I received healing on that day. God took away my rage, all that deep-seated anger that ran deep within me. I write today with this news for you: I am a changed man! Praise GOD!

Twenty years have passed since that weekend, and to this day, I have no rage. I'm happy to tell you that you're safe on any road where I'm driving. Your wife is safe, your children are safe, your grandmother is safe, and your mom and dad are safe on the roads I travel. I am God's representative as I drive on those streets today. In fact, my truck has Jesus' name all over it as I witness His great love on the roads that you and I drive on. And I can tell you this: that kind of healing transformation only comes from Heaven!

* * *

Maybe as you are reading this right now, you're thinking, "Well, I'm not a road rager." And to that I would add, "Let's praise God that you're not." But maybe you're the guy who goes to church on Sunday, and as soon as church is out, your feet hit the pavement, you're heading to your car, and you can't wait to get out of there. You're cutting people off as you're leaving the church parking lot, or maybe it's the Walmart parking lot, or your local grocery store. Maybe you're just a small road rager, not out of control like I was.

Or maybe you're the guy who buries his anger. You might say, "Sure, I get angry, but nobody sees it on the outside." I would venture to say that's just the story you're telling yourself, because believe me: the people who know you the best can tell when you're stuffing your anger and acting like it's no big deal. You probably withdraw from the ones you love the most.

Maybe you go back into your man cave or outside for a walk, or maybe you go hide out in your garage or your toolshed. That's called separation, and Satan loves separation. Every time you separate from your loved ones, Satan is delighted. He wants to isolate you in your own thoughts, your own environment, and away from other believers who can get you back on track. Men, I believe Jesus is weeping while you are separating.

Or maybe you're the guy who says, "I would never pull anybody over in road rage, and I would never touch anybody with my fist. But I'll never lose an argument." Perhaps you're the guy with the sharp tongue who will never lose a verbal discussion. You always come out on top, and you'll do whatever it takes to slice and dice your opponent with your weapon of choice: your words. I think Jesus grieves every time you whip out that weapon: your mouth.

Maybe you're the revengeful type. You don't get angry immediately, but you stew on it. Days or weeks might go by, and all the while your mind is calculating how you'll get back at the one who hurt you. Satan loves that, too. He delights in the time you spend thinking about revenge and retribution.

Men, what kind of anger do you have? I stand before you as a changed man, and you have the opportunity to receive that same kind of healing. But you must be willing to go to the depths of your heart, to do what is necessary to get it out.

Jesus is trustworthy. He is faithful. He will hear your prayer. He will answer you. Why don't you pray right now? Ask Him. God wants to heal your anger.

* * *

Jesus, I thank you that you are a God of healing. Thank you that you can change lives. How do you want me to confess my anger, so that I can be healed and restored? Let there be less of me and more of you, less of my anger and more of your love, your kindness, your gentleness, your patience, your self-control. Meet us. Show me, Lord.

* * *

In your anger, do not sin. --Ephesians 4:26a

Everyone should be quick to listen, slow to speak, and slow to become angry, because human anger does not produce the righteousness that God desires. --James 1:19-20

Fools give full vent to their rage, but the wise bring calm in the end. --Proverbs 29:11

* * *

BE STRONG!

1. Tell the truth. Confess that you DO have anger in your life, and oftentimes it is NOT good because it hurts others (and yourself).
2. When do you feel angry? Time? Place? Situation?
3. Do you have a bodily reaction (head, chest, stomach, fists etc.)?

Be Strong!

4. Where is Jesus in your life when you feel this kind of anger? How can you ask Jesus for help?
5. Are you willing to ask Jesus for help now?
6. Do you need to reach out to others for additional support and help?

Chapter Five
Sadness

Grieving the Losses of Hopes, Dreams, and Relationships

"I want my four hundred dollars back."

My father said that to me. He had given me a Craftsmen tool set, and six months later, he said, "You can send me my toolbox that I bought you as a gift, or you can send me a check for four hundred dollars. But I want my money back." He wanted it because he was so disappointed in me, my kids, and my wife.

I can tell this story now because my dad and I have mended our past. I've changed, and he has changed as well. But the brokenness in our relationship has caused my greatest wound: sadness. I share this story with you from a place of healing, but I remember the sound of his voice and the hurt of that pain.

Father and Son

At the time, every guy who had a garage wanted that three-piece Craftsman toolbox set. It was the real deal, and it was an extraordinary gift from my dad. You see, my dad was conservative with money. He taught me many important things, including the value of money, how to make money, and how to make it work for me. But he was not often generous, aside from Christmas.

Please understand, we weren't poor at all. Our home was old, but it was solid and sturdy. We had plenty of food and I was never hungry. My clothes were clean, and I had shirts for every day of the week—and even some weekend shirts. Life was good. But my parents were frugal with money. So this gift was unexpected, extravagant, and generous.

My mom and dad were visiting our family for the weekend. On Sunday, I needed to catch a flight to Atlanta for my work with Procter & Gamble. I said goodbye to my wife, my two young sons, and my mom & dad, who would depart later to drive home to Texas. Later that evening, I got a call from Debi. In the few hours I had been gone, there had been a falling out between my father and my wife. My sons had been playing basketball in the backyard, and the constant pounding on the concrete was too much for my dad. He stormed outside, he yelled at both of my sons, he punted their basketball over the fence into the neighbor's yard, and then he came inside to tell my wife she was a terrible mother who couldn't discipline her children. My wife called me to say, "He needs to leave the house. He's out of control."

> *But the brokenness in our relationship has caused my greatest wound: sadness.*

I was in Georgia, my family was in Colorado, and that was the starting point of a huge deterioration in my relationship with my dad.

I gave the matter a few weeks of breathing room, but within a month, I scheduled a trip to Texas to meet with my dad to discuss what had happened. I needed to know what had gone on. I needed to know why he would blow up that way in my house with my family—who, by the way, are his family, too.

We met at Denny's restaurant, and he brought my mother. I was surprised to see her, because I thought we were going to have a father-son conversation, man to man and face to face. Things would be different if my mother was there.

We were almost finished with our meal when I said, "Dad, let's talk about what happened a few weeks ago in Colorado."

And all of a sudden, my dad blew up. He leaned across the table, and he said, "I am not going to discuss this in front of your mother."

"Well, I came all the way here so we could discuss this and clean this up."

"I told you, we are *not* going to discuss this in front of your mother. Follow me outside."

That was odd. It was dark outside, and my dad was so angry, and I couldn't imagine why he would want to talk about this outside unless he intended to fight me. I followed him around the back of the restaurant, and I prepared for him to take a swing at me.

We were standing next to the dumpster when he turned to me and said, "Here's how this is going to go. I'm going to do all the talking, and you're going to do all the listening. And I don't want any of the 'Corporate America Communication Skills' crap that comes out of your mouth. You are just going to listen."

He laid into me, pointing his finger in my face and using lots of curse words. He said he had never liked my family. He was tired of my wife, and he didn't want anything to do with her. He only wanted a relationship with me and my younger son, Zach. He never mentioned our older son, Scott, who is disabled. But he didn't want a relationship with him either. Basically, my father wanted to separate me from my wife and my son.

When he finished spewing, I would not be silent. I came back at him. I said, "Twelve years ago, we stood in this town with five hundred people gathered at our church. You heard me speak vows to my wife, and the two became one. Nothing separates me from my wife. *Nothing*. Not even my father."

I will never forget where we were standing: next to the Denny's dumpster. It was so symbolic of the conversation, the garbage he was throwing at me and dumping onto my family. My father was trying to bring death to my marriage, and I would not let that happen. In the face of my defense, he turned and walked away. He couldn't even finish the fight.

He walked away from me and out of my life.

For the next seven years, we had no letters, no visits, and almost no communication. Our relationship with my father was broken; however, I stayed in contact with my mom.

I knew his seventieth birthday was approaching, but my dad and I were not in relationship. My mom called one day and said, "Steve, it's Christmastime, and your dad's birthday is coming. Your sisters are coming, and they're bringing their husbands. It would be great if you could be here."

She did not invite my wife. The other spouses were included, but not mine. I did not know how to mend this relationship with my dad if my wife was not part of the equation. She is part of me.

I didn't give my mom an answer over the phone. I gave it some time, prayer, and conversation with Debi and the men in my soul group of *Marked Men for Christ*. I kept hearing my mom's voice in my head. "He'll only turn seventy once. It will be a surprise for his birthday, the weekend before Christmas. Could you possibly come?" Basically, she was asking *could you get over yourself?*

We concluded, through prayer and Debi's support, that I would go. I would fly in on Friday, and I'd get a hotel and a rental car. I knew I couldn't spend the night in my parents' house; that was far too painful to even think about. I hadn't been to my home town in more than a decade, but I would go.

I would take the first step across this gap between my dad and me.

My sisters wanted to give him the gift of a "specialty" dog, which was a hard gift for me to give. I grew up on the same farm where they grew up, and we all know the farm culture of dogs: they're disposable. They come and go, they get hit by cars, and they get bitten by snakes. When a dog dies on a farm, you get another one. Not only did they want to give our dad a dog, but they wanted me to pay my one-third share of $1,200! It was a hard ask for me, but yes. I was in.

All in, for whatever it took.

We surprised my dad on Saturday morning, and everything went well. He enjoyed the surprises, the dog, my sisters, and our time together. We

> *He laid into me, pointing his finger in my face and using lots of curse words.*

were off to a good start. I went back to my hotel that evening, with the plan to meet at church on Sunday morning. My mom modeled for me the importance of prioritizing God on Sunday morning, and she never missed church. (She still doesn't.) Joining her at church on Sunday was part of the weekend experience.

After church, we went back to the farmhouse for lunch. And that's when things began to fall apart.

While my mom was preparing the table, my dad slipped away to the other half of the house, and I could see him through the glass door. He motioned for me to come to him. I'd seen that finger before, and I knew what it meant: a private, one-on-one conversation.

I walked to him, and we stood arm distance from one another, close enough to touch, but not willing to reach across the brokenness. He pointed his finger in my face, and he said, "You are NOT MY SON. I wasted my time raising you and I'm sick and tired of that religious crap that comes out of your mouth."

WHAT? He kicked me out of his family.

On his seventieth birthday, my father disowned me.

I heard my father deny me as his son, and I felt the pain of an old, familiar rage. I had been healed of my anger for four years by then, but my flesh wanted to hit him.

> *"You are NOT MY SON. I wasted my time raising you and I'm sick and tired of that religious crap that comes out of your mouth."*

But because I am a new creation, I did not respond in anger. I went straight to sadness. Sadness is my greatest wound because my father struggled to love me for who I am. I felt a physical hollowing of my body, a big, gaping hole of sadness from my collarbones to my hips. I couldn't believe this had happened, and I couldn't stay anymore.

I was not welcome in my family's home.

My mom saw us through the glass door, and she came to us. "What's going on? What are you talking about?"

"Well, Dad just kicked me out of the family. He said he wasted his time raising me, he is tired of the religious crap that comes out of my mouth, and he said I'm not his son."

She begged me to stay. My mother wailed, pled, and cried. She longed for me to stay in her home, to stay in her family... to at least stay for lunch.

I wanted to leave, but I love my mom so much. I decided to stay for one more hour.

Somewhere between that moment and our meal together, my mom instructed my dad to speak to me. She asked him to think of something he liked about me. Anything he liked.

He stared at me. I waited in silence, for maybe half a minute. Then he said, "Well, I like how you're not fat. You've kept yourself in shape. And I like how you fix your hair. It's a good style. And your facial hair. I like that."

That's my father. That's all he could say. What shows on the outside is what he appreciated most.

All of my life, I wanted him to see who I was on the inside, but he could only see my work, my athletics, and my grades. How I love my wife, how I love my sons, how I love the Lord, how I lead my family—these did not make him proud of me. He only appreciated that I wasn't fat, I wear my hair well, and I trim my beard.

I left after lunch.

We lived on the tallest hill in Guadalupe County, and on my way down that hill, familiar Scripture hit me again with a brand-new clarity. I thought of the words Jesus gave his disciples: "If anyone will not welcome you or listen to your words, leave that home or town and shake the dust off your feet."[10]

I pulled my car off the gravel road. I got out of the driver's seat. Through tears, I started brushing the dust off my pants and my shoes. I set myself free. And I moved on, out of town.

When I got on the plane to come back home, back to the people who love me for who I am—especially Debi, my sons, and my soul group brothers, I wrote a letter to my Father in Heaven. You see, I was an orphan. Yes, I have a physical father, but he had kicked me out of his family. Maybe he still loved me, but he didn't like me, and he definitely didn't want to be around me or my family. All I had left was my heavenly Father.

---

[10] Matthew 10:14

I realized in that process that I hadn't yet explored my relationship with my heavenly Father. Sure, I'd pray, "Our Father, who art in heaven, hallowed by your name," and I understood the concept. But I didn't have a relationship with him.

See, Jesus and me, we're friends. I don't have the Spirit figured out yet, but I trust in His presence in my heart because I believe in the deposit of the Holy Spirit when I accepted the Lord as my Savior. Jesus and the Holy Spirit were more comfortable for me to wrap my mind around, but I had projected too much of my earthly father onto my relationship with my heavenly Father. I hadn't learned to trust who He was and who He is.

> *So as his adopted son, God has been preparing my whole life for me to know that I am loved.*

So I wrote a letter to our Father, who art in heaven. I said, "I need you. You're all I've got."

With those words, something changed within me. That was the day I felt truly loved and known as the adopted son of the Most High King. Paul reinforced this over and over in his teaching, reminding us again and again that we are adopted into the Kingdom of God. The cool thing about being an adopted son is that adoption is a choice. The father did not become a parent because of a mistaken moment of passion. No, adoptive parents *plan*. They prepare a place. There is a process. So as his adopted son, God has been preparing my whole life for me to know that I am loved.

Just for being me.

I don't have to do anything to earn his love. He just loves me. Truly and completely, he loves me.

I understood this for the first time on that day.

Pain is a great teacher. The awful pain of being kicked out of my family taught me that I am truly loved. I am adopted into God's heavenly family, and on that day, my relationship with my heavenly Father took off.

My life hasn't been the same since.

*   *   *

Jesus, you loved us first. I love you, too!
You told your disciples that if we knew you, then we would know the
FATHER.
Thank you, for showing me the perfect Father's love. It has changed my
life—forever.
I pray for the men who are reading this,
that they too will have an AWESOME relationship with our Father who
is in Heaven! Give them the wisdom and strength to do whatever it takes to
receive the Father's love.
Amen.

*   *   *

"God decided in advance to adopt us into his own family by bringing us to himself through Jesus Christ. This is what he wanted to do, and it gave him great pleasure." --Ephesians 1:5 (NLT)

"God sent him to buy freedom for us who were slaves to the law, so that he could adopt us as his very own children." --Galatians 4:5 (NLT)

"The Lord is close to the brokenhearted and saves those who are crushed in spirit." --Psalm 34:18

"The human spirit can endure in sickness, but a crushed spirit who can bear?" --Proverbs 18:4

"If anyone will not welcome you or listen to your words, leave that home or town and shake the dust off your feet." -- Matthew 10:14

*   *   *

BE STRONG!

1. Read John 11:17-44 and remember that Jesus experienced the loss of His friend Lazarus. Look at the way He responded to deep loss.
2. Who or what have you lost in your lifetime?
3. Write down your loss or losses. Talk to Jesus about what is going on in your heart.
4. Share with another what you have discovered about your loss, grief, and the hope you have in Christ.

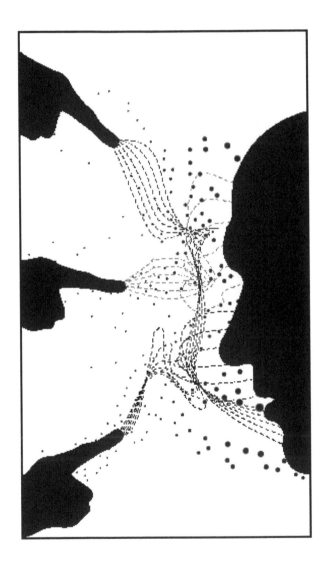

Chapter Six
Shame

"Not Good Enough"

Shame is humiliating.

Shame is a painful emotion caused by our conscious awareness of guilt, poor decisions, or a personal shortcoming. It is a sense of "less than" or "not good enough." Shame is evidence of something to be regretted.

Shame is not part of God's design for us. In fact, in the story of God's creation of Adam and Eve, Scripture tells us that Adam and his wife were "both naked and they felt no shame" (Genesis 2:25). When sin entered their lives, shame entered as well. Adam and Eve began to cover themselves; that's the key to shame: we cover it up.

Most men feel a degree of shame. We feel like we are not good enough, so we are always working to prove that we are smart enough, fast enough, quick enough, and strong enough. In fact, we have a favorite American cliché: "I may not be the smartest one in the room, but I'll work harder than anybody here." We love phrases like that one.

Or, we'll say, "I may not be the strongest, but I'll give 110%." It's a lie. What percentage did Jesus give? He gave 100%, and he gave his whole life. So it's impossible to give more than Jesus gave, and it's not even possible to give a full 100% as long as you're still breathing with more to give. But shame is a great motivator, and we will promise more than we can deliver.

Shame is a two-edged sword. One side reflects those who have shamed me, and the other side of the sword reflects those whom I have shamed. Both sides of that blade are painful and awful.

In this chapter, I want to look at both sides of the sword of shame in my life, and I'll explore its consequences from three angles: in my family, in my marriage, and in ministry.

Shame in my Family: Wounding my Sons

In 1986, my wife Debi and I had been married for four years when she became pregnant with our first child. We didn't know if this baby would be a boy or a girl, but it took me no time at all to compile a long list of dreams for this child who would be my firstborn. I daydreamed about having a son or daughter, and my dreams were specific: nothing but the best for this child. *If it's a boy*, I thought, *I hope he'll be bigger than me. I tried out for the NFL, but I couldn't make it. My son? He'll start in the NFL. He'll be better than his father. College was a workout for me, but I did it. My son? He will be more intelligent than me. I only have one four-year degree, but maybe he'll have two.*

> **"I may not be the smartest one in the room, but I'll work harder than anybody here." What percentage did Jesus give? He gave 100%, and he gave his whole life.**

Maybe he will have a master's degree and more. My son will accomplish more than his dad could. He'll build on my foundation. He will do more than me. As a new dad in my early twenties, I had the greatest hopes.

In October, my wife gave birth to our first son, and I was thrilled. I was with her for the delivery. We didn't have any family in the area, and we hadn't made many close friends yet. It was just my bride and me in the hospital. I sat on the side of the bed next to Debi, and we waited for the nurse to bring us our baby boy. I was in shock and awe over what my bride had just endured, all that had happened, this whole experience. There is nothing like the overwhelming moments of becoming new parents.

The door opened, and the nurse appeared, holding our son in the crook of her left arm. I remember that she was pointing to his face with her right hand. With an abrupt tone, she said, "I've been a maternity nurse for more than two decades, and I've *never* seen a child look like this before."

She thrust the baby at us. And that was our introduction to our first son, Scott.

You see, when Scott was born, he looked like he was 120 years old. He was gaunt. With no fat in his face or his body, he was bony like a skeleton and wrinkled like an old man. As the nurse said, she had never seen a baby like this one. That's because, we later learned, Scott had a rare chromosome abnormality. When the Human Genome Project included Scott's DNA in their worldwide research of the mid-1990's, Scott's specific chromosome abnormality was the first that the science world had documented. We all have our own thumbprint and DNA structure, but Scott's anomaly was at that point the only one recorded in the world. Our son is unique.

Here's how that plays out for my son: Scott is in his early thirties now, and he is mentally delayed. If you were to look at him, you would see that he looks like his father, a mini-me, but he has some physical differences. He walks differently, and he talks differently. He speaks as if he might be deaf, but he can hear. He has oral apraxia, so he cannot form language or pronounce words like a normal person can. His mind is like a young teenager, but his body is that of a fully grown adult. Scott can read maybe fifty words. He cannot manage money. His short-term memory is not good, and neither is his long-term memory. He needs adult care and supervision every day.

Scott's physical sensation of touch and feel are different from what is normal. Scott does not know if he's hungry or not. If you mention food, he'll assume it's time to eat, but not because he's necessarily hungry. And when he is finished eating, he may not know if there's food on his mouth. If he has body odor, he cannot smell it. His body doesn't perform like an average person of his size and age.

But the beauty of Scott is this: *he is okay with who he is*. It's his father who struggles with who he is.

For many of the more-than-thirty years that Scott has been alive, his father has carried shame. I have needed to learn to be okay with Scott when he doesn't wipe his mouth when he finishes eating, or when he doesn't care for himself in the bathroom, or when he doesn't put on deodorant. Scott is okay with

> *But the beauty of Scott is this: he is okay with who he is. It's his father who struggles with who he is.*

Scott; it's his dad who struggles. Learning to love my son—as the person he is—has been a three-decade work project for me.

Since the day the nurse presented Scott to us, I have often asked God why He gave Scott to me. The answer is this: God gave me Scott to teach me how to love and forgive.

Let me tell you what is beautiful about my son. He has joy every single day. He has always been delighted to see me. He forgives almost immediately. In fact, Scott's gifts are forgiveness and love, just for who you are. I do not have to perform to receive Scott's love, because Scott simply loves. It's who he is. He accepts others for who they are, not for what they do.

Scott has never had a bad day in his entire life. How many bad days have I had in the last three decades? Too many to count.

My son is a gift from heaven. And he teaches me every single day.

You see, Scott is not six feet tall, bulked up with muscle, tipping the scales at 275, and playing for the Dallas Cowboys. Although he didn't make it to the NFL, he's an all-star on Jesus' team. He loves with an agape love.

His father is still trying to learn how to do that.

I have a second son, and his name is Zach. He is also a younger version of his father, but in a very different way. Zach has the beauty of my wife Debi, but he has the heart and spirit of his dad. Extremely masculine, outdoorsman, and a hunter. He has worked in the oil field and in construction, he graduated from Colorado State University with a degree in construction management. Zach is married to Katy, whom he loves very much, and she is a great gift to him and our family. The world is wide open to possibilities for him.

But Zach does not do life his father's way.

You see, I had a path laid out for Zach: I envisioned him working for a big corporate firm in the construction world. I knew he could become very successful with the powerful engineers who build high rise buildings and construct interstate highways. This is a great industry, especially in America. I wanted him to be under the umbrella of a corporation with all the financial benefits they can offer their employees.

He tried my plan. He actually worked for two of the top five builders in America, and he did well. But it's not what he wanted.

Zach longed for the entrepreneurial world, and he wanted to be his own boss. He has started several companies on his own.

I wish I could tell you that I applauded his independence, but the truth is, I felt really disappointed in him. He wasn't doing it my way. I thought he was wasting his time, talent, and treasure by being his own boss and starting his own company.

Unfortunately, I shamed my son.

I shamed him with my words when I told him I thought he could do better. I didn't encourage him to continue on the path he was on, and I sent a clear message that I believed he had made a mistake. I told him he should stop what he was doing, go back, and get a job with a big company. I thought my heart was in the right place by offering him wise counsel, but I now see that I only wanted him to do what I wanted him to do. I was more concerned with him doing it my way, instead of letting him find his own way. I wounded my son, and I created a gap in our relationship.

Last year, Zach and I were planning to go hunting together in a neighboring state, and I knew that these three hours together in the front seat of our truck would give me just the opportunity I needed to apologize to my son. I needed to repair the damage I had done.

I made a navigational error in our drive: when I exited the interstate, I should have gone south, but I went north. While we were looking for our spot, unaware that we were on the wrong path altogether, we were entering hour number four of the drive. This seemed like a good time to confess to Zach my regret and my sorrow, a good time to ask his forgiveness. I opened up my heart and I told him how sorry I am for telling him what to do. I made a promise to accept whatever career path he chooses. If he needs help, he can ask me, and I will give him any help he needs. But I won't call the plays for his game. I will stand ready to assist in whatever plays he wants to call for the game of life that he is in.

Zach, being the strong man he is, came back powerfully. He agreed with me that I had been wrong, and he wasn't too quiet to tell me how he felt about it. He told me how my words affected him, he told me what he didn't like, and he accepted my apology. He forgave me.

The timing was remarkable.

You see, after about thirty minutes of driving north, all while having this dialogue with my son, I realized I was driving in the wrong direction…much like I had taken our relationship down the wrong path. Both physically and metaphorically, we turned around. I remember feeling speechless over what the Holy Spirit had done. The healing that had happened in the front seat of that truck was far beyond anything I could have orchestrated.

That hunting trip changed me.

On this trip, Zach was the one with a hunting license, and I became his outfitter. I paid for gas. I organized the details. I was the camp cook. He brought his gun and his license, and I took care of the supporting details. We took a strong turn that week. I had a sacred chance to show my son, "Let me support you: your plan, your route, your victory."

Now I am a cheerleader for Zach. Once I became aware, I could begin the necessary repairs so he would not have to carry that wound. I love him, and I want every success for him on the path he chooses for his career.

I don't need him to be like me. I need him to be Zach.

And I want to love him for who he is, just for being Zach.

Shame in My Marriage: Wounding my Wife

The most important relationship for a married man is with his wife. That's my first ministry. Everything else is secondary.

Scripture tells us that a good leader of God's men must first take care of his own family before he can care for anyone else, so that principle is true for me and anyone else who has a ministry outside their home. As a married man, my relational priorities must fall in this order: my wife, my children (when they need me; adult kids don't always need us), and then everyone else outside my home.

Men, we must take care of the individuals in our home first.

> *Now I am a cheerleader for Zach. Once I became aware, I could begin the necessary repairs so he would not have to carry that wound.*

I've been married for almost four decades, and I love my wife more than I could write in this book. Still, in my sin, I shame her. One of my sins is lust, and I shame my wife every time I look at another woman with an elongated stare, whether it happens in her presence or not, whether she sees my glance or not. An elongated look at another woman shames my wife.

I shame her when she makes a mistake and I remind her of it.

I shame her when I keep a list of wrongs.

I can shame her with my actions. And I can also shame her with my inaction.

For example, I shame my wife when I don't tell her how beautiful she is, any time it crosses my mind. I shame her when I don't tell her that I love her, multiple times a day. When she does something to serve me or our sons and I fail to thank her, I bring shame to my wife.

Inaction lets the recipient wonder about their worth.

Inaction can lead a wife to wonder, *Am I enough? Do you care for me? Did you notice? Do you love me? If he didn't say it, then I'm probably not enough.* A woman's mind goes to questioning. Shame is something regrettable; inaction makes a woman wonder if she is regrettable. When I choose to bless or to love her instead with my words, I can erase that wonder of regret. It is a choice, and I can choose to love with intention, with my words, and with my actions.

Shame in Ministry: Christians Shaming Christians

Shame cuts two ways, and both edges cut deeply as we give and receive shame. As I flip the sword over, I can recall who has shamed me in painful ways. Some of the worst shame I have known has come from other believers. You see, I spent more than thirty-two years in corporate America, and it's a dog-eat-dog world out there. But even compared to that world of landmines, the most painful wounds can happen inside the church. How it must break the heart of the Jesus when we wound one another with shame, and yet we do this to our brothers and sisters who bear His name.

A few years into the public ministry of *Marked Men for Christ*, John Lager and I faced accusations over and over again. A couple of men went on a local radio station and shamed us publicly. One man gave a speech in a neighboring state, recorded it, and posted it on a website. Once something is on the internet, you can't get it off very easily. The attacks seemed relentless, and it didn't stop with those few.

In 2010, I joined a neighborhood church in my city. I was attracted to the biblical teaching of their lead pastor, and I invited him to join us for a *Marked Men for Christ* weekend. He had a life transforming experience—so much so that he in turn invited many of the men on his staff. Three of his men attended a Phase One experience, but their response was different. Using their skills with technology, they created a page that mocked *Marked Men for Christ*. They included a special section directed straight to me, mocking me. They made fun of my name, the way I talk, and the words I say during a Phase One ministry experience. On the day that website launched, phone calls and emails were flying into our headquarters. I've been called some crazy things out in the world by those who have never even been in the ministry, but I was shocked to see this kind of abuse. They shamed the ministry, they tried to shame those involved, and they personally and publicly shamed me as the leader of *Marked Men for Christ*.

One of the negatives of being the point man of a global ministry is that people love to take shots in the public forum. The person on the front lines takes a lot of hits, and it's a painful privilege to bleed on the front lines of God's ministry. A good analogy is a warrior's spear. A spear needs the entire length in order to be effective, but the entry point of the weapon is the bloodiest part of the tool. Not the back, not the middle, and not six inches behind the tip. The tip of the spear is the most bloodied because it enters first and travels the deepest distance inside its target. The analogy is gory and graphic, but it is illustrative and true. A spear demonstrates the degree of pain a leader experiences. When God wants to use someone like me to be the point man and the face of His ministry, I become the tip of the spear. I am not the whole spear; I'm just the tip. It is a privilege and an honor to be the tip of the spear, and I thank Jesus for how he has changed my life by this chance to serve. And being the tip of the spear means I'm going to take a lot of hits. It is probably true for the lead pastor of any church, as well as any ministry leader who is willing to be vulnerable and lead.

Among the thousands of members we have within *Marked Men for Christ*, there are many gifts; some of our members have gifts with technology. Someone took that website down within a day, and they rerouted the link! So when a person would click on that link, it actually took them to the home page for Disneyland! I didn't ask anyone to act on my behalf, but God moved with justice and protection. It's good to have a tribe, and the Holy Spirit was my protector and my shield.

I should tell you: I am a warrior, and confrontation comes naturally to me. It is in my nature to be ready for a fight, to protect, and to defend. Sometimes this fleshes out in ways that are not honoring to the Lord, but God is continuing to use this tendency to train me. Fortunately, before I confronted the men who made this website, a board member of *Marked Men for Christ* reminded me of Jesus's teachings about how we are to confront our enemies. He reminded me that Jesus said, "Love your enemies and bless those who persecute you" (Matthew 5:44). I was strengthened by my friend to confront them in love. God loves them as much as He loves me.

So, I confronted them in love. I didn't raise a hand, though I could have. I didn't hurt anybody with my strength, though I was hurt deeply enough to want to. I didn't commit any acts of retaliation or retribution. They each apologized, and I spoke my forgiveness to them. It is one thing to say the words, "I forgive you," but it is another to feel the peace of forgiveness as truth in your heart. That comes only through the healing power of God, and I praise Him for that maturation and sanctification.

> *I forgave them, though the wound cut deeply.*

Jesus modeled this love on the cross. Love is a choice. It is not easy, and it is not natural, but it is a choice to love like Jesus loves. The fruit of forgiveness is His.

I forgave them, though the wound cut deeply. It hurt even worse because it was born of relationship. With this particular wound, I no longer feel the pain, but I do have a scar. It is similar to a scar on my arm from fifty years ago. I can look at that scar on my forearm, the size of a fifty-cent piece, and I can recall how that flesh was torn. I don't want to experience that again, and neither do I want to experience that pain of mockery and ridicule in my own church. Just like physical wounds, emotional and relational wounds can heal but the scar remains ever present.

The question we must ask ourselves is this: when you recall the shame others have heaped upon you, is that memory still an open wound, or is it a healed scar?

Jesus Can Heal Our Shame Wounds

When correcting someone's choice or actions, I have often heard one person say to another, "Shame on you!" I want to be honest with you: I hate those words. I imagine Satan loves those words, because he loves for us to live under a dark shroud of shame.

But Jesus never spoke that way. He only spoke truth with grace and forgiveness.

Think of the woman at the well. She was alone at the well because she had been ostracized from her community. She had been covered in shame. But Jesus met her there, and He called out her sin in truth. The Perfect Man spoke to one of the most shameful sinners, but He never said, "Shame on you." With His grace and forgiveness, He healed her shame. First, she saw Him as a prophet, but later in the chapter, she confessed that He is the Christ. He is the Messiah. In fact, it's possible that she was the first female evangelist, aside from the mother of Jesus Christ. This woman at the well ran back to her village to tell people that she had met the Messiah. She longed for them to know Him too.

How much hope this can give us! No matter how much shame the public can see, Jesus can use you to be an evangelist to speak His Good News. Nobody wanted to be associated with her except for Jesus, but He healed her broken heart. He used her to be a light to the world. Essentially, He said, "I choose this one." He wanted to use her. And He can use us too.

That truth should give us all hope.

* * *

Lord, I need help to heal, and I believe You offer the healing I need.
If we don't ask for the healing of our shame, then it does not come.
I ask you to take away my shame today.
Transform my open wounds by Your power and for Your purpose.
I ask you to make me aware of my actions as well as my inactions,
that I may not be the cause of shame in the life of anyone else.
Thank you for your healing power, Jesus. Amen.

* * *

"You have heard that it was said, 'Love your neighbor and hate your enemy.' But I tell you, 'Love your enemies and pray for those who persecute you." --Matthew 5:43-44

But to you who are listening, I say: Love your enemies, do good to those who hate you, bless those who curse you, pray for those who mistreat you." --Luke 6:27-28

* * *

BE STRONG!

1. Think of both sides of the sword of shame in your life. First, who has shamed you? Who are the enemies who have hurt you? Jesus tells us we are to love our enemies and bless those who curse us. Bless them today. Pray for them by name and with a heart of compassion.

2. Who have you shamed? How have you shamed others, in public or in private? With your words or your thoughts? What actions do you need to take to repair any shame wounds you've created?

3. The healing of shame begins with an awareness. We get it out of our consciousness by speaking it or writing it. If you are alone, write it down. If you are in a small group, let's speak it out loud. Take action to get this shame out of your heart.

4. Take a stand today and decide that you will not use the words "shame on you." Let's make that something we choose never to say to one another, that we may not wound each other with our words.

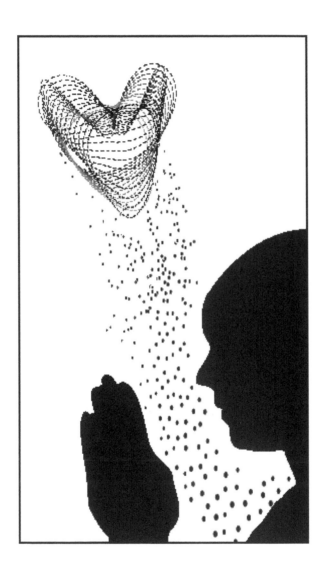

Chapter Seven
Forgiveness

Giving and Receiving Forgiveness

When my father told me that I was "not his son" and that he had "wasted his time raising me," the wound within me was so deep and raw. Even a year later, I felt like I had a gaping hole in the core of my body. The pain didn't go away, but life didn't stop happening either. My children were growing, my wife and I were tending our marriage, I had a professional career to maintain, and I was leading a growing ministry. I was a wounded leader.

In this season of intense emotional hurt, we hosted a leadership event for our core leaders of *Marked Men for Christ*. It was the first night of a three-day experience, and things weren't going well for me. I was so tense, and my tension was affecting the whole team.

I got up to go to the bathroom, and when I came back, I noticed the men were circled up in a meeting. An unplanned meeting. Now, at that point, my leadership style was to "command and control." If I didn't command that meeting, it should not be happening.

I stormed into their circle with anger that was big and loud. I demanded to know who had called this unauthorized, unsanctioned meeting. I interrupted their conversation, and I shut it down. There would be no more meetings, no more gatherings tonight. I sent everyone to bed. Everybody was uncomfortable. I yelled at them, these men who were my friends and the best leaders of the organization. It was not right, it was not justified, but I was hurt.

Hurting people hurt people.

Forgiveness with Others

I lay down in my bunk. It was February in Colorado, and we were at an elevation of 8,000 feet. I woke up in the middle of the night, and I had to relieve myself. There was no bathroom or running water in the bunkhouse, so I had to go outside in the dark, freezing cold with the snow on the ground. I started praying while I relieved myself under the moonlight.

God, I am so angry. I am so broken. What I did was wrong. But I am so hurt. In fact, I'm angry. I am angry at YOU. When are you going to heal this hole in me? When are you going to show up?

I felt silence in the air and in my spirit as I went back into my bunk. I fell asleep, and in my sleep, I had an encounter with God. He met me in my pain.

I had a vision of Jesus. He was probably ten feet away from me, and he was kneeling on one knee in the dirt. He had his finger in the dirt, just like He did when He met the woman caught in adultery who had been caught in sin and shame. I don't know what He was doing in the dirt, but He wasn't looking at me. I could see myself in this dream, and I could see the outline of my body with a giant hole in my core, from my collarbones to my hips. My heart was so broken.

I started screaming at Jesus. "Jesus! When are you going to heal me?!" I pointed to myself, to this big hole in my chest.

Jesus kept his head down. He spoke calmly and evenly, and He said, "I'm not going to heal you now. You want me to tell you

I'm proud of you. I won't do that now. You want me to give you a hug. I won't do that now. But Steve, know that I love you."

"Yes, Lord, I know that you love me," I said, but I couldn't wait for His healing.

I started screaming His name again, louder this time. "Jesus! When are you going to heal me?!"

He still didn't give me any eye contact. He chose not to look at me, but He replied again in a calm voice, "Steve, I am going to heal you. But not now. Even though I won't do it now, know that I love you."

"Yes, Lord, I know that you love me," I replied again. The third time I spoke His name, it was not through screaming, but through my tears. "Jesus, when are you going to heal me?"

And the Lord said to me in my dream, "You want me to get up off the ground, come over there, look you in the eyes, give you a big hug, and tell you you're going to be okay. I am not going to do that. But you need to do that to those men you've hurt. They do not

> *I started screaming at Jesus. "Jesus! When are you going to heal me?!" I pointed to myself, to this big hole in my chest.*

need your unstated expectations upon them."

He never looked at me.

He didn't give me what I wanted.

He kept His eyes in the dirt, and He was calm and gentle. He heard everything I wanted, and He answered every prayer.

But He would not give me what I wanted.

I woke up at 6:00 in the morning, and I called a meeting. I didn't tell them about my vision during the night, but I told them God had spoken to me and told me to apologize. I confessed to each of those guys, man to man. I said, "I am sorry. I was wrong. I hurt you. Please forgive me." I apologized to each man, and I promised to change.

I wish I could tell you that all of the men offered me their forgiveness immediately, because most of them did. Unfortunately, two of the men did not accept my apology. Even as I write this, they still may have not forgiven me. One man has left the ministry, and that grieves my spirit. We are friends, but I know I hurt him. Even though I apologized, I could not erase the hurt. There was one other who did not forgive me in the moment, and though I did not appreciate it at the time, I see the wisdom in his withholding. He said, "I am not going to give you what you want right now. You want me to accept your apology, but I am not ready to. I will not do that yet." He wanted me to continue to grow, and you cannot grow by getting your way all the time. I see the wisdom in that decision. There are consequences for the ways we treat one another, both in the good and the bad.

That was in 2005, more than a decade ago. God continues to heal me from my anger, and He continues to heal that hole within me. I want to say He has healed me completely, but there is still some scar tissue around those wounds. They are there so I can remember the pain as well as the massive healing that has taken place.

Forgiveness with My Dad

Just this past year, I was in North Dallas for a ministry event, and I chose to visit my dad. My sister invited me to come, and there was some anxiousness about why I would want to visit. But I wanted to take a step to close the gap between my dad and me.

During my visit, my dad and I went out to the garage together. He said, "Stay here, I have something for you." I thought he was going to give me some of his artwork, as he is an artisan of mosaics. But he came back holding a shotgun, and he held it out with open hands.

Let me step out of the story for a moment to explain my affinity for this. I spent most of my childhood growing up in Texas, and I have a long history as an outdoorsman and a hunter. Hunting is something fathers and sons do together, and I have an emotional conviction that a father should give a gun to his sons. *I've done this multiple times with both of my sons.* My two sons know that they will one day get my collection of guns, and it's important to me, this legacy. So when my dad came to me in his garage, and he held out this gun for me to take, he was speaking right to my heart.

> ***Don't you remember, Steve? This gun was yours from the beginning. It's always been yours."***

He said, "This gun is for you. It's yours."

"No, Dad," I said, "That's your shotgun. That's the very first one we bought when we moved to the farm in 1970. Don't you remember?"

"No, don't *you* remember? That's not the story. I bought this gun before we left Florida when you were in fifth grade. We went to the sporting goods store, and I told the guy at the counter, 'We just bought a farm in Texas, and I need for my son to have a gun that's his size. A first timer's gun. What would you recommend?' And he recommended this single-shot twenty-gauge shotgun. Don't you remember, Steve? This gun was yours from the beginning. It's always been yours."

It's always been yours.

Those words were sweeter than a latte from Starbucks. They went down so smooth. Those words are so biblical, and they offer an invitation.

I hear in my mind the words Jesus gave in the parable of the Workers in the Vineyard.[11] On the equator, they work from 6:00am to 6:00pm, from sun up to sundown. In this story, the master went into town at 6:00am, and he took his servant with him. At this early hour of the day, he said to the townspeople, "Who wants to go to work in my field today?" Some of them joined him, but it wasn't enough. At 9:00, he went back, inviting more to join him. At noon, he invited more. He does this again at 3:00 and again in the last hour of the day, at 5:00. He offers five invitations throughout the day, each one saying, "Come. Let's get to work." At the end of the day, the master pays everyone, and he pays them all the same.

Jesus taught this story to His disciples to show us that God loves us all the same. He paid all of his workers the same amount, and He loves us all with the same love. It's all about choice. Choose to say "yes" to His invitation, the sooner the better. God invites us, "Come, and you'll be blessed. Whether you come at the first invitation or the fifth, you will receive my love, and my love will be for you the same as it is for everyone else."

Here's the difference: the guy who showed up at 6:00am had been receiving the love, grace, and forgiveness of God for eleven more hours. We may have each heard the invitation at the same time, but some of us wait until the very last hour to receive it. That's why it's so good to come on the first call: it doesn't mean more love, but it does mean more time with Jesus.

There's an invitation there for you. He is waiting with a gift that has always been yours.

---

[11] Matthew 20:1-16

Forgiveness: The Gift that has Always Been Yours

That shotgun my father gave me is probably worth sixty dollars. But it is precious to me. It represents grace and love and forgiveness. There was a time, in my adult life, when I had nothing to say to or about my father. Now I can look back to that leadership retreat in 2005. Jesus said He would heal me, but not in the time and the way that I wanted the healing. He asked me to trust him. He said, "You can trust me, Steve. I will heal you."

And all these years later, He healed my heart with the words from my dad. "It's always been yours."

I saw the fruit of the Holy Spirit in my father on that day. I had spent time with him, and he gave this gift to me. When we give and share the fruit of the Spirit, the fruit multiplies. Those dividends were paying back. Someday, I will speak at my father's funeral, and I look forward to the day when I can share the good news of how my father finished his life strong. I will talk about how he shared those sweet words with me, "It's always been yours."

* * *

Jesus you are amazing! Your grace and glory are abundant.
We pray for fathers and sons, that their relationships may be STRONG.
We ask for sons to honor their fathers,
and we ask for dads to love their sons with great grace and understanding.
Lastly, we are reminded that we are all adopted sons into the heavenly
family. This is an amazing grace! We thank you, JESUS!
Amen.

* * *

"Be on your guard; stand firm in the faith; be courageous; be strong." --1 Corinthians 16:13

"...who forgives all your sins and heals all your diseases." --Psalm 103:3

"And when you stand praying, if you hold anything against anyone, forgive them, so that your Father in heaven may forgive your sins." --Mark 11:25

"...Forgive, and you will be forgiven." --Luke 6:37

* * *

BE STRONG!

1. Who do you need to forgive? That person who hurt you – what is his or her name?
2. Do you feel resentment or maybe are still holding onto the pain? Read: Matthew 6:14-15.
3. Can you remember the scar (healed wound) and still offer forgiveness to someone?
4. Share a part of your heart with a trusted friend or spouse. Then pray together and simply ask Jesus to heal your open wound or your scar of remembrance. Trust in HIS healing and restoration (Isaiah 53:5).
5. Never forget: Know that you are the adopted son of a most high God. You have two fathers; you are the son of an earthly father as well as our heavenly Father. Keep your identity in mind.

Chapter Eight
Holiness

You are a Holy Man

Picture a birthday gift: a wrapped box with six sides: top, bottom, and four side panels. What you see on the outside may be nothing special, or it may be beautifully wrapped. It could be wrapped in shiny paper and tied with a bow, or it could be wrapped in the sports section of the newspaper secured with duct tape. Gifts come in all shapes and sizes, and some are attractive to look at, while others are not. But you and I both know, we are most interested in what is on the inside. That's where the good stuff is. The real gift is not the wrapping, but the secret that's tucked inside.

Holiness is like this. God's people are like wrapped birthday gifts. Some are more attractive on the outside, and they're polished to shine. You can look at them and see they've spent time preparing themselves before they stepped into the world. Others are rough around the edges, and they show up like the tattered page of the sports section in the newspaper. Jeans, sloppy, didn't shave – they don't look great. It doesn't matter. The real gift is on the inside. You see, God lives inside His people. He dwells within us, and He is the gift we carry.

Holiness in You

Do you believe that Jesus Christ is the Messiah? I hope you will say yes. And do you believe that He lives inside you, that He abides in you, that He has taken up residence inside your person? I hope you said yes to this as well, because it is the truth! The Spirit of truth lives inside you and me, and Jesus told us this repeatedly throughout Scripture:

> "I will ask the Father, and he will give you another advocate to help you and be with you forever—the Spirit of truth. The world cannot accept him, because it neither sees him nor knows him. But you know him, for he lives with you and will be in you" (John 14:16-17).

> "Jesus, replied, Anyone who loves me will obey my teaching. My Father will love them, and we will come to them and make our home with them" (John 14:23).

> Again Jesus said, "Peace be with you! As the Father has sent me, I am sending you." And with that he breathed on them and said, "Receive the Holy Spirit" (John 20:21-22).

He's actually going to live with you.

Those are the words of Jesus Himself. This may cause some resistance within you, and it may be a message you're not used to hearing. After all, our culture wants to put men down. We receive messages every day that put men down, telling us we are trash, we're animals, we're no good, and we should be more like _____ (fill in the blank). This is wrong. God made us differently. He made us in his image, to be like Him, to bear His name, and as His followers, He calls us holy.

We are more accustomed to hearing how sinful we are, right? And we are sinful. It's a true statement. Yes, I am a sinner, I am broken, I need a Savior. I need Jesus. I cannot save myself, and I need the One who died for my soul. But I am also called to be like Christ. Jesus is the goal. He is holy, and He has given me his Holy Spirit, so I may live a holy life. I can live in holiness, I can avoid sin, and I can make choices to live as Christ lived.

That doesn't mean I won't sin, but it does mean that I choose to sin less often and in less duration. I am still a broken man, but

> *He has given me his Holy Spirit, so I may live a holy life.*

my life looks totally different than it did before I became a saved believer. Before I was saved by Christ, I would just keep on sinning. Because why not? I was living in ignorance. And maybe it didn't feel good the next minute or the next day, but there were no rules or boundaries for the actions of my spirit.

Now that I am a Christian, Jesus is my model. He shows me what it means to be a man who is holy and without sin. He is my goal. And this holiness is for all who believe: men, women, Jews, Gentiles. We see holiness mentioned when Peter talks to the Jewish nation, and we see holiness in Paul's letters to the people of Corinth, Rome, and Ephesus. All over the world, believers are called to be His holy people.

As you continue to read this chapter, open your mind. Yes, you are a sinner—saved by grace. Hallelujah! Now you are called, as an anointed believer in Christ, to live a holy life. He is the resurrection, the Messiah, and He has made His home in each of us. Since that is the case, God has called you holy. Without stain, blemish, wrinkle, or fault. Because of Jesus' sacrifice, and because of your belief in Him as the Savior of the world, God sees you as holy.

What is holiness?

In Scripture, the word *holy* is used in three different ways. The first is with the word *sanctified*, which means to be set apart or declared as free from sin. The second is with the phrase *separated*, which means we are set apart from this world because of Christ and the indwelling of His Spirit. And the third use of *holy* refers to a calling or anointing on your life. The only way you can live your life as a holy person is through Christ.

In the Amplified Bible, we find these words from Jesus, talking about His disciples in the world:

> Sanctify them in the truth [set them apart for Your purposes, make them holy]; Your word is truth. Just as You commissioned *and* sent Me into the world, I also have commissioned *and* sent them (believers) into the world. For their sake I sanctify Myself [to do Your will], so that they also may be sanctified [set apart, dedicated, made holy] in [Your] truth.[12]

The gift of sanctification does not happen overnight; it is a process. He is making us holy every day, and it's an ongoing work. The Scriptures gave us several word pictures to demonstrate this process, and these examples are both agricultural and physical. First, in a physical word picture, Paul wrote about the physical challenges of running in a race. In his letter to Corinth, he wrote, "Do you not know that in a race all the runners run their very best to win, but only one receives the prize? Run your race in such a way that you may seize the prize and make it yours!"[13] God wants us to stay in this marathon. This life of ours is a race, and we are meant to win. We do not run aimlessly, and we do not box at the

---

[12] John 17:17-19 AMP
[13] 1 Corinthians 9:24 AMP

air. No, Paul said he was beating his body, making it his slave. He confessed that he was one of the worst sinners of all, and he had a calling to preach the Good News. He stayed in the race, so he would not be disqualified from the prize. That's how God wants us to run, acknowledging our sin and pursuing holiness. As we give ourselves up to the Lord, we become more like Jesus. This is holiness.

In an agricultural word picture, Jesus told us that He is the vine and we are the branches.[14] On Day One of any planting project, the branch does not produce any fruit. But over time, through the days and nights, through the sunshine and the rainy season, that branch that remains connected to the vine produces fruit that can be shared with others. It happens *over time*. As long as you stay connected to the vine, as long as his words and truth flow through you,

> *The only way you can live your life as a holy person is through Christ.*

then you are on a path to holiness. As Christians, we will reap the benefits of a life of holiness, and Paul describes these benefits as the fruits of the Spirit: love, joy, peace, patience, kindness, goodness, faithfulness, gentleness, and self-control.[15] He has said that a branch that does not produce fruit, one that is apart from him, will dry up and be set apart to burn.[16] They are worthless as ashes. But as long as you and I stay connected to Christ, the vine, we will produce beautiful fruit. This is holiness.

Take Holy Action

---

[14] John 15 NLT
[15] Galatians 5:22-23 NLT
[16] John 15:6 NLT

So then, since God sees me as holy, and this holiness is confirmed in Scripture, how do I live my life as a holy man? How can you be a holy man in your home, in your work, in your family, and when you are all alone?

First of all, know your identity. Know who you are. I know that I am the adopted son of a most high God. That's who I am. I am a man, and I am the son of my earthly father as well as my heavenly Father. I must keep that identity in mind.

> *Know who you are. I know that I am the adopted son of a most high God.*

Second, know who you are on the inside. I am a temple of God Himself. This body is a holy temple, and I carry God wherever I go. I am a representative of Him in the world, and my actions should reflect the Holy One who lives in me.

Third, I need to know my weaknesses as well as my strengths. This makes me well equipped for my spiritual battle today. God's enemy is my enemy as well because I am aligned with the work and the will of Jesus Christ.

Satan has one purpose: to steal, kill, and destroy everything God has created—including me. Satan wants to speak lies into my heart and mind, because he has a mission today: to take me out. When I keep a fresh awareness of who I am, who I belong to, who lives inside me, and the weaknesses that can distract me from holiness, I can make healthy decisions that model the love of Christ in my life.

Holiness begins with offering my body and my life as sacrifice. Paul wrote in his letter to the Romans, "Therefore, I urge you, brothers and sisters, in view of God's mercy, to offer your bodies as a living sacrifice, holy and pleasing to God—this is your true and proper worship" (Romans 12:1).

Your call is to be holy. In God's eyes, we are a beautifully wrapped gift. He is in us, and He wants us to produce beautiful fruit.

This is holiness.

*   *   *

Jesus, you are holy!
You call us to be like you.
We need help to achieve this, so you send the HELPER, the Holy Spirit!
Thank you, LORD!
Amen.

*   *   *

I am the Lord, who brought you up out of Egypt to be your God; therefore, be holy because I am holy. --Leviticus 11:45

For you are a people holy to the Lord your God. The Lord your God has chosen you out of all the people on the face of the earth to be his people, his treasured possession. --Deuteronomy 7:6

Therefore, as God's chosen people, holy and dearly loved, clothe yourselves with compassion, kindness, humility, gentleness, and patience. --Colossians 3:12

Therefore, I urge you, brothers and sisters, in view of God's mercy, to offer your bodies as a living sacrifice, holy and pleasing to God—this is your true and proper worship. Do not conform to the pattern of this world, but be transformed by the renewing of your mind. Then you will be able to test and approve what God's will is—his good, pleasing and perfect will. For by the grace given me I say to every one of you: Do not think of yourself more highly than you ought, but rather think of yourself with sober judgment, in accordance with the faith God has distributed to each of you. --Romans 12: 1-3

* * *

BE STRONG!

1. Can you accept the truth that God has made you holy? Finish this sentence and speak it aloud to another person: "My name is _____, and I am holy because of what God has done for me." Say it, hear it, and believe it.

2. Ephesians 5:3 says, "But among you there must be not even a hint of sexual immorality, or of any kind of impurity, or of greed, because these are improper for God's holy people." Identify the sin that is currently keeping you from holiness. Finish this sentence, and then speak it aloud to another person: "My name is _____, and I am holy because of what God has done for me. I am dying to this sin _____ more and more, and I seek to live more righteously through the power of the Holy Spirit. Amen!"

3. Husbands, there are specific words for our holiness in the Bible. Ephesians 5:25-27 says, "Husbands, love your wives, just as Christ loved the church and give Himself up for her to make her holy, cleansing her by the washing with water through the word, and to present her to himself as a radiant church, without stain or wrinkle or any other blemish, but pure and blameless."

4. Ask yourself, what actions should you start doing around your wife or others? What should you stop doing around your wife or others?

5. Which of the following holy attributes is most lacking in your daily life? Which one can you seek to sharpen?

- o Compassion
- o Kindness
- o Humility
- o Gentleness
- o Patience

Remember: You are a holy man.
Be holy as He who made you is holy.

Chapter Nine
Mission

"What Is Your Life All About?"

Many years ago, back when I had two jobs, I had to travel on airplanes on a regular basis—many planes every week. On this day that I am recalling, I was flying to Las Vegas. It was just another day, like any other day of business travel. I woke up, put on my "monkey suit," grabbed my laptop, and I headed off to the airport. Nothing special, just another day.

I had been to the airport so many times that I had an airport routine, from the parking lot and through the security lines. I had a routine for the airline flight as well. First, I would get out God's Word, and I'd spend some time reading the bible as the plane took off. Then, once we'd reached optimal elevation, I'd listen for a bell to go off, giving me permission to use my electronics. Then I'd put my Bible away, get out my laptop, and get to work. An hour and 15 minutes later, as we would descend into Las Vegas International Airport, another bell would go off to signal all passengers to shut down our electronics. That's when I would begin my third phase of the routine: reading a book.

At that time, I was reading *Wild at Heart*, by John Eldredge. It's a very good book, and I was at that part where the author is talking about God's mighty men. I remember how desperately wanted to be one of God's mighty men, but I wasn't. I was afraid. Afraid of not knowing enough, not being good enough, not having enough time. I knew God had a bigger purpose for me, but I didn't know what it was, and I was afraid of what it could be. So I played small for God. I felt so convicted of this awareness that day, and I was just writing and writing in my journal as the plane landed. God had given me so much to think about, and I wanted to capture those thoughts while they were fresh.

Now, normally I'm one of the first people off the plane. I drink a lot of coffee, I chase it with a lot of water, and let's be honest: when the plane lands, I need to get to the restroom. But that day, I was so busy writing in my journal that I wasn't the first off the plane. That's where my routine began to change a bit that day. The decision to stay in my seat put me in a different place at a different time, which turned out to be just where I needed to be.

I know Las Vegas International airport like I know my way around my own neighborhood, and I know there are two restrooms in terminal D. I know all the junior travelers go to the first restroom, but the more seasoned travelers go to the second one. We who travel often know there are fewer people down at the second restroom. It's less crowded, there are shorter lines and far less people likely to mess with my stuff.

> As a guy ran past, he called out, "We've got a man down! I'm going for help!"

In the men's room, I was up against the wall, doing my business, when suddenly I saw a flash of movement behind me. As a guy ran past, he called out, "We've got a man down! I'm going for help!"

I finished what I was doing, and as I turned around the corner, I saw that there was a man laying down on the floor inside the stall. He was motionless beside the commode. I opened the door and I knelt down next to the man. I'm not a doctor and I'm not medically trained, but I had taken a Red Cross Lifesaving Course a couple of years before. I knew where to check for his pulse but couldn't find it. Maybe it was because I didn't know what I was doing, or maybe it was because he was a large guy and I wasn't pressing hard enough, but I couldn't find his pulse. I feared he didn't have one.

He was motionless, and he made one sound. Like a quiet grunt. He made that sound a couple of times.

I took out my phone, and I called 9-1-1. I said, "Ma'am, I'm in the Las Vegas International Airport. I am in terminal D, in the restroom closest to baggage claim. We've got a man down. Motionless. Before I called, he was making a sound, but since I've called he has stopped making any sounds."

"Sir, what's the address?" she asked.

"Ma'am, there's only one international airport in Las Vegas. Terminal D, like David. Please send help."

"We're on our way."

As I put my phone down, the man who had run past me was now standing there next to me. I turned to him and I said, "Do you know Jesus?"

He threw his arms up, like he didn't know who I meant. He shook his head no.

I said, "Now's a good time to start talking to him."

I turned my attention back to the man on the floor. I gently moved the man's head away from the commode. I tilted it back. I pinched his nose. I reached into his mouth to move his tongue aside and clear his airway. I put my mouth over his mouth, and I blew my breath into his body. I got immediate feedback. His body immediately responded.

If you were watching this from the outside, you might have thought, *Wow. Look at that great guy trying to save that man's life. What a hero.*

But you couldn't know what was happening inside me. I was scared. You see, I sold professional cleaning products to dirty places. Las Vegas has a lot of filth in their hotels, which made this a perfect market for my company to send me in to clean it up. I knew a lot about bacteria and viruses, so I knew that the floor of a public men's restroom is one of the nastiest places on the planet. Just kneeling on that floor was nauseating to me. It took a lot for me to push through that fear.

Here's what else I knew: the second dirtiest place on the planet is the human mouth. I didn't know this guy on the floor. I didn't know if he had HIV or a herpes virus. It was possible that he could vomit while I was trying to help him, and I'd have his vomit in my mouth.

I had a whole lot of fear. I needed a whole lot of Jesus.

So yes, I helped him, but I held back. It might have looked good from the outside, but only I knew that I didn't do everything I could do. If you're doing mouth-to-mouth resuscitation, you have to give it everything. I didn't. Only I knew that I didn't do a complete lip lock on the man. I held back just a little bit. It just felt weird to me. I'm married to my high school sweetheart, I'm a heterosexual man, and I am not attracted to dudes. And here I had to put my lips on another man's lips. I needed the strength of Jesus to do the right thing.

Praise the Lord that we serve a God of second chances. Not just two chances, but seventy times seven. In my spirit, I heard God say to me, "Do it again."

So I did it again. And this time I gave it my VERY BEST effort. A complete lip-lock. I breathed my breath into him. I did chest compressions. Over and over and over. I handed my phone to the guy standing next to me. "Call 911 again," I said. "Get those EMTs here."

I kept moving, doing mouth-to-mouth and chest compressions, repeating the cycle of lifesaving measures. All of a sudden, I felt pressure on my shoulder. It was an EMT. *Finally.*

The EMT pushed me out of the way, and he pulled the man out of the bathroom stall and into the open space of the bathroom. Two more EMTs arrived, and together they got to work. The first guy had a pair of scissors, and he cut right through the man's $50 dress shirt and $40 tie. He peeled his clothes back to expose his chest. The second EMT put a needle into the guy's arm. The needle was connected to a bag with fluid in it. They handed me the bag, and they told me to hold it high. I watched as they worked, and I prayed for the guy on the floor.

> *It was possible that he could vomit while I was trying to help him, and I'd have his vomit in my mouth. I had a whole lot of fear. I needed a whole lot of Jesus.*

The third EMT opened a box and he took out two pads. He flipped a switch on the box, coursing electricity through the paddles. He raised the pads, and he yelled, "Tone" He slammed the paddles onto the patient's chest, and the electricity coursed through that man's body. It looked like his body came six inches off the ground.

He did it again. "Tone!" *Boom!*

I was holding the bag, looking down at this guy on the ground. He was about my age. I saw that he had a ring on his finger. So, he's married, I thought. And I wondered, what were the last words he said to his wife before he went to work this morning? What did he say? Did he tell her that she's the most beautiful woman in the world? Did he tell her that he knew God had made her just for him, and that their lives were better together than they were apart?

Did he tell her how beautiful she is, that she fulfills every need he has? Or did he shame her? Did he tell her that she's getting a little fat? Or maybe she's aging and her skin is changing and she's getting a little ugly and loose. Maybe he's going to buy her a terrible birthday gift, like a gift certificate to 24-Hour Fitness so she can trim down and tone up a bit. What were the last words he told her this morning?

I wondered if he had any children. Did he have a son? What were the last words he told his son before he went to work? Did he tell him how proud he was? Did he tell him he was a reflection, not only of his mother and father, but also of his heavenly Father? Did he lift him up and encourage him? Or did he tear him down and rip him to pieces? Maybe he said he wasn't good enough, not smart enough, not a hard-enough worker. Maybe he shamed him because he didn't go to church enough. Maybe he said that the way he talked sounded terrible and ignorant, or that his attitude toward life was irresponsible. Maybe he told him his work ethic was lazy. What did he say to his son?

What if he had a daughter? Did he tell her she's beautiful? A princess? Did he take time to give her special time away, dinners or day trips, to model what it's like to be a holy man in a household? Did he give her an example of a godly man, to show her in advance what to look for in the man God had chosen for her to marry? Or did he rip her to pieces and shame her because of her behavior? Did he tell her she's ugly, she hangs around with the wrong crowd, and she's damaged goods? What were the last words and messages that his daughter heard from him?

The guy was getting up in age. He probably had twenty years or more invested in his career. Maybe he was planning for his retirement years. Maybe he was looking forward to some fishing, a little cottage in the hills, or a boat on the lake. Maybe he planned to finally go on that vacation he always wanted. Maybe he's holding back a little on his dreams, because he's working hard on his career path and he just needed more money. *So much for his retirement,* I thought. *This guy may not even see lunch today.*

They worked on that guy for at least twenty minutes, all three of the EMTs. Then they pulled the needle out of his arm. They took the pads off his chest. They got a big piece of plastic, and they wrapped it around his body. They zipped his body up into a bag. They picked him up and put his body in the bag on the cart, and they wheeled him out of the men's restroom in Terminal D of the Las Vegas International Airport.

Today wasn't just another day for him, or for me.

How many breaths do you have left? Take a guess. A hundred thousand? A million? Maybe a hundred million?

Go ahead and take one. Inhale, exhale.

That's minus one more.

Only God knows how many we have, and it's not as though He has a vague idea. He knows exactly how many each one of us has left. And on that day in the Las Vegas Airport, as that man breathed the last breath that came out of his body, it didn't belong to him. It belonged to me.

How many breaths do you have before God asks for the last one back? How will you spend your days, your moments, your breaths?

We are God's holy people, set apart to do His will. But how can we know what His will is? What is God's will for you and me? When I woke up today, there was a reason. Breath is a measure of time, and we receive a gift each time air fills our lungs. God gives us that breath, and He gives it with a reason and a purpose: He has something for each of us to do.

What is that purpose? Am I to simply wake up, inhale oxygen, exhale carbon dioxide, consume food, and create waste?

Or is there a purpose and mission for my life? A unique calling?

The book of Romans tells us that I am chosen and set apart, sent out to do God's will. And so I must believe that there is a mission, an anointing, and a call.

Jesus' Mission

I think we can all agree that Jesus came not just to inhale oxygen, exhale carbon dioxide, consume food, and create waste. He had a much bigger purpose. In fact, He was prepared for three decades before he revealed his mission to the world.

> *How many breaths do you have left? Take a guess. A hundred thousand? A million? Maybe a hundred million?*

In the fourth chapter of the book of Luke, Jesus is teaching in the synagogue in Nazareth. He's talking to church people—folks like you and me—who have already believed in Jesus as the resurrected Christ, Messiah, and Savior. They didn't know this guy was the Savior, but they believed in God and they believed what He had promised would be true. They had the law, they had the prophets, and so you would think that these people were an ideal audience for Jesus. He stood up to read, and He opened a scroll from the prophet Isaiah. Unrolling it, He read these words:

"The Spirit of the LORD is on me,
because he has anointed me to proclaim good news
to the poor.
He has sent me to proclaim freedom for the prisoners

and recovery of sight for the blind,
to set the oppressed free,
to proclaim the year of the Lord's favor."[17]

Then, the passage tells us, Jesus rolled up the scroll, gave it back to the attendant, and He sat down. The story says that every eye in the synagogue was fastened onto Him, and He said to them, "Today this scripture is fulfilled in your hearing."[18]

He had just read to them his mission, his anointing, and his calling. He explained why he was born.

Let's break it down into smaller pieces to see how this applies to us. First, he said, "The Spirit of the Lord is upon me," and we know that, as believers, we have this in common with the Son of God. He has anointed each one of us, and we have been called out.

To do what? Well, next Jesus said He was anointed "to bring Good News to the poor." He has sent you and me to bring His good news to anyone who hasn't heard it yet. They may not be poor with finances, but they may be poor in spirit. And Jesus asked us to show them the better way.

Next, He said He had been sent to proclaim that "captives will be released, that the blind will see, that the oppressed will be set free." Most of us have eyesight; we are not blind. But He's not talking about what we can see with our eyes; Jesus is talking about what we can see with our hearts. We can see and believe where we are headed, and though we cannot see the one in whom we place our faith, we love Him with our hearts. When He talks about captives and prisoners, He's not talking about people who are in physical jail cells, but rather people like you and me, imprisoned

---

[17] Luke 4:18-19
[18] Luke 4:21

by our sin. Our sins keep us locked up, as prisoners to our bad decisions. Jesus came to set us free, and His gives us the authority to share that freedom with others.

Finally, He said He was here "to proclaim a year of the Lord's favor." That's not a calendar year; it's a season of time. We are in a season of God's favor. He loves us so much, and He has given us this time to serve Him, know Him, and share His name with all who will hear. He showed us His mission, and He is our model.

The Mission of the Disciples

At the end of Jesus' physical ministry here on earth, after He had been crucified and raised again to life, He brought together His disciples in Galilee. Just before He departed to heaven, He said to all of his men:

> "Therefore, go and make disciples of all the nations, baptizing them in the name of the Father and the Son and the Holy Spirit, and teaching them to obey everything I have commanded you. And surely I am with you always, even to the end of the age."[19]

Again, just as we looked at Jesus' own mission, we can break down this commission that He gave to his disciples, and we can apply it to our lives. Let's do this, one phrase at a time.

First, Jesus said, "Therefore, go." Don't you just love that solid beginning? To live out my mission, I can't stay seated in front of the TV in my La-Z-Boy recliner. I can't fulfill my mission if I'm lying in bed at 10:30 on a Tuesday morning. He's telling us to *go*. He's asking us to *physically move*. If you have a body that moves,

---

[19] Matthew 28:19-20

take action. If your body has failed you, then take actions with your thoughts and in your heart. But whatever you do, *go*.

He said, "Go and make disciples." How do we do that? It's a slow process that takes time, and it involves interaction with people. We need to spend time with them, one on one, face to face, knee to knee. Invest your time in people, focused on Christ with Scripture, prayer, and a heart of compassion.

You can do this in person and individually, but in this day and age, you can also make disciples through your use of social media. Post Scripture on Facebook or Instagram, Twitter or SnapChat. Write a brief reflection on prayer or post some thoughts on the fruits of the Spirit. Use your phone to text a prayer to someone. Maybe they needed that exact encouragement today, and you have the resources to speak into the life of that person. We have so many tools and resources that empower us to take action to help make disciples.

Then, Jesus commissions the disciples to "baptize them in the name of the Father and the Son and the Holy Spirit." If you have ever had the privilege of baptizing a fellow believer, then you know what a tremendous blessing you receive when you baptize someone else. Even if you have not been granted this gift, you do have the opportunity to come alongside someone who is not a

> *Live life as a holy man. Live in mission for Jesus and with Jesus until He calls you home.*

believer, and you can encourage them in the process as they commit their lives to the Lord. Romans 10:9-10 tells us exactly the steps of choosing a life with Christ: "If you declare with your mouth, 'Jesus is Lord,' and believe in your heart God raised Him from the dead, you will be saved. For it is with your heart that you believe and are justified, and it is with your mouth that you profess your faith and are saved." Is this something that you need to proclaim right now? If yes, speak aloud to JESUS – right now! And may God bless you as you choose to trust in Him!

Finally, He says, "teach them to obey everything I have commanded you." To teach them, you come alongside them. Not as one who is ahead or above them, but as one who can walk with them to share what you know about Scripture and your relationship with Jesus. Speak from your own experience. Model love, forgiveness, and compassion. Be a grace giver. Know that you have been blessed so you can bless others, and in this way, you can teach others to obey what Jesus has commanded.

Your Mission

We can be sure that God has been preparing you throughout your childhood, teen years, and young adult years to begin to step into your mission, just like Jesus did. You and I are disciples of Jesus Christ, so our mission must be pretty closely aligned with His. As you look to define your mission, consider these passages. These verses offer a list of ways we have been entrusted with the gifts of the Holy Spirit.

There are different kinds of gifts, but the same Spirit distributes them. There are different kinds of service, but the same Lord. There are different kinds of working, but in all of them and in everyone it is the same God at work. Now to each one the manifestation of the Spirit is given for the common good. To one there is given through the Spirit a message of wisdom, to another a message of knowledge by means of the same Spirit, to another faith by the same Spirit, to another gifts of healing by that one Spirit, to another miraculous powers, to another prophecy, to another distinguishing between spirits, to another speaking in different kinds of tongues, and to still another the interpretation of tongues. All these are the work of one and the same Spirit, and he distributes them to each one, just as he determines.

1 Corinthians 12: 4-11

We have different gifts, according to the grace given to each of us. If your gift is prophesying, then prophesy in accordance with your faith; if it is serving, then serve; if it is teaching, then teach; if it is to encourage, then give encouragement; if it is giving, then give generously; if it is to lead, do it diligently; if it is to show mercy, do it cheerfully.

Romans 12: 6-8

God has blessed you—specifically and individually *you*—with gifts and talents. You are called. You are anointed. You are holy.

Your mission is your target. Lock in like a laser. Know your gifts and your brokenness and keep them both in front of you. Live a life of awareness. Live life as a holy man. Live in mission *for* Jesus and *with* Jesus until He calls you home.

* * *

Jesus, you modeled a life of conviction.
You were "ALL IN" and you gave your very best.
Help us to be MORE like you, and less like us!
Help us to know our gifts, our life mission and have the wherewithal to live
it FULLY ON every day until you call us HOME!
Amen.

Be Strong!

*   *   *

"Therefore, go and make disciples of all the nations, baptizing them in the name of the Father and the Son and the Holy Spirit, and teaching them to obey everything I have commanded you. And surely I am with you always, even to the end of the age." --Matthew 28:19-20

"The Spirit of the LORD is on me,
because he has anointed me to proclaim good news to the poor.
He has sent me to proclaim freedom for the prisoners
and recovery of sight for the blind,
to set the oppressed free,
to proclaim the year of the Lord's favor." --Luke 4:18-19

*   *   *

BE STRONG!

1. Pray. Ask the Lord to reveal your gifts to you. Ask Him to show you your mission with this life you've been given.
2. Look at the verses above. Consider the gifts and talents listed. From those, what do you believe are your top three gifts?
3. My mission: "I am Spice, and as a marked man for Jesus Christ, I co-create a loving world, by modeling the love of Jesus with; great faith, wisdom and holiness!" Begin to formalize your mission into a sentence, just as Jesus did before the synagogue. He put His mission into words from Isaiah, and you can put your mission into words now as well. Begin with this phrase: "As a believer in Jesus Christ…"

4. Memorize your mission. Commit it to memory. You can begin to filter your actions and decisions through this mission statement, and you can determine whether you are on mission in your daily life.

Chapter Ten:
A Commission and an Invitation
A Word from the Co-Founders

How did the ministry of *Marked Men for Christ* begin?

Steve "Spice" Spicer

If someone asked you to choose two men out of a crowd, with a plan to pair them as partners to go into ministry together, you likely would not put us together at first glance.

John is a Roman Catholic priest. Officially, he is Reverend or Father John Lager, a Capuchin Franciscan Friar. He has been a friar for forty-six years, a priest for forty years, he lives in community, and he follows the rules of St. Francis. If we met for breakfast, he would likely be in street clothes, but he often wears robes and a collar. Spend 5-minutes with him, and you know he's holy.

And somehow, God put him with me, "Spice," a bearded guy dressed in camouflage and a baseball cap. I'm a former Division I football player, grew up on a Texas ranch, and a retired executive from corporate America with more than three decades of climbing the ladder to the corner office.

But with the help of our mutual friend, Mel Claytor, God brought us together for a vision far greater than we could have ever imagined.

John Lager

We met twenty-six years ago when a fellow Catholic priest was scheduled to lead a retreat, but he got sick and cancelled. Mel had been with me on a retreat I had done years before, so he gave me a call. The circumstances that led me there were both accidental and providential, as it was my first encounter with Spice. It was a powerful weekend and a grace moment! From that weekend, we've been leading men's ministries together ever since. It's been an amazing blessing to me to share the gift of ministry in this great partnership.

A few years into leading together, our friend Gary was diagnosed with stage four melanoma cancer. Devastated by this news, we knew this would be a journey that would teach us much. He battled the disease for five years, and in the last two and a half years, we were intensively and intimately involved in his care. As we cared for our friend, walking him to his death, we watched how he dealt with his own brokenness. He was a young man in his early forties, married with young children. The challenges were many. His journey was the catalyst that helped us to learn how to be sensitive to the needs of men, and we gained an understanding of exploring a man's heart condition. We began to understand the elements of true relationships among men: being transparent and speaking truth.

After Gary died, Spice and I were making a trip to Kansas together to serve some leaders in ministry, and we were mourning the death of our friend. We had been together for three or four days, and we were finally on our five-hour drive home. It was gray and windy, and there was nothing but tumbleweed around us. All of this time together allowed a deeper conversation: "Where are we going? What are we going to *do?*"

Spice

I was in the front seat of that car as we explored this conversation about a ministry for men, and I felt God impress a clear message onto my heart: *I want you to do this.*

What should we name it? It was very important to both of us that the ministry not be named after ourselves, and we did not want to create a new company. This idea and this ministry would belong to Christ. He gave us the idea, he gave us our experiences and the gifts of many others who would partner with us, and this ministry would be HIS. We came up with the name *Marked Men for Christ.*

We created a list of the five main wounds men carry throughout their lives: deceit, anger, fear, sadness over losses, and shame. Men experience other wounds as well, but these are the Core Five. We wanted to not only explore the wounds of men, but to also lead them to the Lord's healing. We desired to help men understand their purpose, mission, gifts, and talents. We wanted to incorporate wisdom from older men and elders in the community.

And before long, we had the tenants of *Marked Men for Christ* mapped out on a legal pad of paper.

John

We asked five men to join us, which gave us a scriptural seven. We wrote the initial charter in December 2001, and in March 2002, we had our first board meeting with these seven men: our original board of directors. We planned the very first Phase One Experience of *Marked Men for Christ.*

A Phase One Experience is a 44-hour journey with the core purpose of building stronger men for Jesus Christ. We begin by helping the men to identify their weaknesses. After all, if you want to become stronger, you must first know where you are weak. After we follow the five wounds into the depths of our experiences, then we begin an ascent upward as we focus on the healing power of Jesus Christ. We focus on how we are strong.

We finish with new beginnings, new hope, and healing from these wounds. We commission the men into their families, work, church and ministries with the knowledge that they have gifts God wants them to invest in others. We equip them to watch the wonder of spiritual multiplication, as each man shares his gifts with others.

Spice

On that first weekend, we saw the power of what God can do in 44 hours. (Though, to be honest, it stretched closer to 70 hours that first time around!) Even now, we can look back and see the essential pieces God put in place from the start. We knew we had something God had truly anointed. In November of 2002, we opened *Marked Men for Christ* to the public, and we hosted our first weekend in Bailey, Colorado.

We maintained two principles for the first five years. First, we committed to keep 80% of what works, and fix the 20% that needs changed. After each experience, we sought feedback from the men who went through the program. We took their perspectives to heart, we prayed about it, and continued to improve. We still continue to tweak the weekend in small ways, but the ministry is truly focused on holding onto the fundamental vision that God laid on our hearts.

Our second principle was this: *Get Strong, then Big.* We resisted the urge to have big events or to spread ourselves out too fast. In the midst of that deep growth, we began to see the fruits of our experience. Through its strength and impact, it became far bigger than the two of us. The Lord raised up among us some truly committed men whom we wanted to commission to become co-leaders.

All of our weekend staff are volunteers, and the leaders have been through a two-year training process to become certified to lead. After they complete the training, they become junior leaders and then senior leaders. Now, eighteen years later, we are approaching 50 men who are certified to lead a *Marked Men for Christ Phase One Experience*. These leaders are all around the world: Africa, Europe, the United States, and we recently expanded into Korea and other parts of Asia.

What started as two men has now multiplied to over 11,000 men!

The road has not been easy, and we have navigated a lot of criticism. In 2003, in our first year of public operation, we were asked to meet with two strangers for a meeting to discuss *Marked Men for Christ*. At the end of a casual lunch, these two men started grilling us on the theology and practices of the ministry. It felt like an interrogation. They railed us with questions: "Who are you? Who gives you the authority to do this? What church are you from? What gives you the right to do what you do?"

Well, the short answer is Jesus. He both called and confirmed the two co-founders to go and do this. We're not tied to any denomination, and we are not affiliated with a specific church. And we don't want to be. We really want to be a faith strength camp for God's men.

God ordained this work, and we are doing what God has ordained.

At the end of the questioning, before we parted ways in the parking lot, I said to the lead interrogator, "Brother, why don't we pray about this? If you're so concerned that this is not of Christ, then let's ask him to stop it. I'll go do something else, whatever God wants me to do. I just want to be in His will." He was willing to pray with me then and there. The prayer was basically this:

"Jesus, if you want *Marked Men for Christ* to continue, then let it continue. If you want it to stop, then tell us to stop. Show us how to stop, and we will obey. Amen."

Here we are, a decade and a half later, going strong. Clearly, God did not want this ministry to end in 2003. Some men have come and stayed since day one. Other men have served for a season and then moved on. We are building stronger men, first and foremost in their relationship with Christ, knowing Christ personally, feeling and knowing his forgiveness, and then empowering the men in the gifts the Lord has given them. As of 2019, men have come from over 2,200 different churches on four continents around the world. He asked us to go and serve, and that's what we've done. It's what we will continue to do until he tells us we are finished.

> *This is where men can thrive and experience radical transformation through the power of the Holy Spirit.*

Marked Men for Christ is not your typical men's retreat. The experience is masculine, intense, and powerful—three qualities men crave, but they have a difficult time finding a safe place to experience them. Churches make people feel safe, but typically men won't take off their masks if women and children are present. Knowing this, *Marked Men for Christ* ministry purposefully creates an environment where they *are* safe. This is where men can thrive and experience radical transformation through the power of the Holy Spirit.

The Phase One weekend is experiential. We expect to experience radical transformation through the power of the Holy Spirit. You won't sit in a classroom and have someone teach you from the front of the room. There will be no keynote speakers or fancy PowerPoint slides. Instead, we set up a biblically-based protocol that will allow you to confess your brokenness through an intentional process.

Then we will pray—and God will heal. He's the one who makes the transformation. We just follow what the Scripture says in James 5:16: "Therefore confess your sins to each other and pray for each other so that you may be healed. The prayer of a righteous person is powerful and effective." We stand on that Scripture and God's promise of healing through prayer after confession (speaking the truth).

Do you want to be STRONGER man for Jesus? If you choose to join us for a 44-hour Phase One Experience and our follow-up 11-week program with *Marked Men for Christ* ministry, you can anticipate four things:

> You will be **Challenged** to look at your life as a man today, and to remember your experiences from past decades that brought you to this point in time.
> You will be **Encouraged** to seek God's strength and healing of any broken areas of your life.
> You will **Grow and Mature** in your faith as a follower of Jesus Christ as you discover the gifts, talents, and blessings from God.
> You will **Connect with other Men** who seek the healing power of the Holy Spirit. We are called to become the Body of Christ as we strengthen one another in love, service, and generosity.

Please consider joining us at a Phase One Weekend, that you may find the healing the Lord has for you. To sign up, please visit www.markedmenforchrist.org.

BE STRONG!

Therefore confess your sins to each other and pray for each other so that you may be healed. The prayer of a righteous person is powerful and effective.
--James 5:16

Be STRONG!

21 Daily Devotions for the Making of a *Marked Man for Christ*

1. Wisdom

2. Coaches, Mentors, and Spiritual Fathers

3. Jesus Sees Your Faith

4. Be a God Pleaser (not a Friend Pleaser)

5. Hardships (Be Encouraged)

6. What Did You Lose?

7. 4th Quarter

8. Let's Pray Together

9. Are You a Follower?

10. Faith Moves Mountains

11. Who am I?

12. Why Do I Have Enemies?

13. Who Is Wise?

14. Work Out?

15. Life is a Journey

16. Grace

17. I Want to be Worthy

18. Making a Deposit of Great Value

19. Spiritual Attacks are Real

20. Fear is a Choice

21. Must Love

Day 1
Wisdom

If any of you lacks wisdom, let him ask God,
who gives generously to all without reproach, and it will be given him.
--James 1:15 (ESV)

Intelligence and **Wisdom** are not the same thing.

To gain intelligence, we can go to school, read books, study, and learn. Intelligence can be available to anyone who is willing to invest the time. But a person can have many years of schooling, multiple degrees, and decades of on-the-job training, and yet that does not mean he has wisdom. Why not? Because wisdom is attained differently. It is extremely valuable and precious, and a gift to receive rather than a skill to acquire.

The demands of your job, the perspectives of your friends, and the influences of the media and culture often place a high value on being smart or intelligent, but Scripture says that wisdom is MORE valuable than strength or weapons.

- **Wisdom** is better than weapons of war. (Ecclesiastes 9:18a) (ESV)
- All the same, I still say that **wisdom** is better than strength. (Ecclesiastes 9:16a)

Most of us would enjoy having MORE wisdom in our lives!

How do we obtain more wisdom? It is easy: simply pray and ask God!

- If any of you lacks wisdom, let him ask God, who gives generously to all without reproach, and it will be given him. (James 1:15) (ESV)

And here is good news: you do not have to be old to be wise. Yes, it may help to have lived many years on the planet, but it is not a prerequisite to having godly wisdom.

- It is not only the old who are wise, not only the aged who understand what is right.
  (Job 32:9)

If wisdom and intelligence are different, how do I know if I have **heavenly wisdom** or **human intelligence**? The Bible gives us guidelines to know the difference.

- *Who is wise and understanding among you? Let them show it by their good life, by deeds done in the humility that comes from* **wisdom***. But if you harbor bitter envy and selfish ambition in your hearts, do not boast about it or deny the truth. Such "wisdom" does not come down from heaven but is earthly, unspiritual, demonic. For where you have envy and selfish ambition, there you find disorder and every evil practice. But the* **wisdom** *that comes from heaven is first of all pure; then peace-loving, considerate, submissive, full of mercy and good fruit, impartial and sincere. (James 3:13-17)*

* * *

BE STRONG!

1. Pause for a moment to discern if you need more wisdom from heaven in your life. If you can have more wisdom, where would you apply it? Consider each of the following areas.
   a. Marriage
   b. Work
   c. Father
   d. Ministry
   e. Other circles of your influence

2. If you desire more wisdom from heaven, then quiet your mind now by taking a few deep breaths. Ask our Father, who loves you, to give you wisdom for this area in your life. Ask Him to

show you areas where wisdom is lacking. Ask Him to show you where you can grow.

3. Now, using a pen and paper or your smart device, write down what God just placed on your heart. Write down His answer to your prayer.

4. Now that you have heard from heaven, what are you going to do?

PRAYER

Jesus, we call upon you and ask for WISDOM from Heaven! Specifically, we ask for what is written in;

> *But the wisdom that comes from heaven is first of all pure; then peace-loving, considerate, submissive, full of mercy and good fruit, impartial and sincere. (James 3:17)*

Lord, we ask for all 8-elements. Thank you, for hearing our prayer. Amen.

Day 2
Coaches, Mentors, and Spiritual Fathers

Whoever walks with the wise becomes wise.
--Proverbs 13:20 (ESV)

In this book, I have shared the painful story of my father disowning me on his 70th birthday. I was hurt and heartbroken, but my heavenly Father had not abandoned me. He showed His faithfulness to me in a new way.

You see, shortly after the incident with my dad, I attended the National Coalition of Men's Ministry (NCMM) conference in Denver. I was leaving the morning session when I saw the president of NCMM is standing nearby. I approached him and introduced myself. He asked about my experience in the conference, and if the ministry was serving my needs. I told him it wasn't going well for me, that I had not found what I needed yet.

"Why not?" he asked.

I look him in his eyes and stated the new truth of my life. "My earthly father recently disowned me. He's dead in my life, and I need help."

Receiving my words, he looked up and shouted over the crowd of men who had gathered. "Chuck, come on over here," he motioned, and a man joined our conversation. "Chuck, this man's father recently died, and he needs a new dad. You're it."

In that moment, God gave a new mentor to me. Chuck became my spiritual father.

Chuck is about thirteen years older than me. He's a man's man, army ranger, lieutenant colonel, PhD and ministry leader. Chuck does not play small. For twelve years now, Chuck and I have met regularly for a time of sharing and growth. This man boldly challenges me, speaks to the deep pain in my soul, and tenderly loves on my heart. He was sent by heaven to provide a "father's love" to Steve "Spice" Spicer, when my heart was broken and rejected by my own dad. Praise GOD!

I continue to seek God's healing as I do my soul work. I desire to model Jesus' love in my life. I invest time reading Scripture multiple times per day, and I continue to confess my personal brokenness to other men and then pray for healing (James 5:16). Guess what? God answers prayers! He heals the broken hearted. My earthly dad has received forgiveness from both God and me. I have invited myself back into his life. I have changed, and my earthly dad has changed. God is healing each of us.

Here is some evidence of the fruit of the tree. Eight years after my father disowned me, I called him on his 78th birthday. Here's the transcript of our conversation, a dialogue different from ever before:

> Me: *How are you and Jesus doing?*
> Dad: *Great.*
> Me: *Excellent! Jesus doesn't change, but we do.*
> Dad: *Yeah, that is true. Jesus is like a big oak tree in a cow pasture, with His limbs or arms stretched out wide for everyone.*
> Me: *Dad, for your 78th birthday gift, may I simply offer to pray for you to Jesus?*
> Dad: *Sure.*

And then, I prayed for my dad, asking Jesus to bless him, to bless his marriage to my mom, and to give each of them strong health in Jesus' name. AMEN! Praise God!

Do you have a Coach or a Mentor who can speak to your heart?

Do you have an older, wise man in your life? Do you have someone who is a good listener and can speak words of life into your heart? Do you have a mature male figure who can coach you up when you get down on yourself or on life?

This man should be probably at least seven to ten years older than you and should be someone who has earned your respect based on the way he lives his life. He most definitely has Christ-likeness, although he's not perfect. Barnabas was a coach and mentor to Paul, and Paul represented this leadership to Timothy. Who is your Barnabas or Paul in your life?

I've been blessed to have several older mentors and coaches in my life, and I think of them as "spiritual fathers." These men help guide me to the path of God's healing and restoration.

God sent a new father to me. He can send a new father to you as well.

Remember your leaders, who spoke the word of God to you.
Consider the outcome of their way of life and imitate their faith.
(Hebrews 13:7)

*   *   *

BE STRONG!

1. Do you have a mentor, coach, or spiritual father in your life?

    a. If you do, GREAT! Take a moment now to thank God that he's in your life and pray for his continued growth and wisdom. Consider sending a text, an email, or a note to thank him for his role in your life.

    b. If you do not, that is okay. Take a moment to bring this request to God. Pray and ask Jesus to send someone into your life who can be your coach, mentor, and/ or spiritual father.

2. Could you serve as a mentor, coach, or spiritual father to a younger man in the faith? Ask the Lord to bring that person to your mind. Somewhere there is a Timothy looking for a Paul. Be the courageous man to start that conversation with a young man looking for a leader.

3. Is there anyone whom you need to forgive today from hurts of the past? Remember what Jesus said to his disciples:

For if you forgive other people when they sin against you, your heavenly Father will also forgive you. But if you do not forgive others their sins, your Father will not forgive your sins. (Mathew 6:14-15)

PRAYER

"Jesus, I want a pure heart. The truth is, I'm like a dryer vent (try not to smile!) with lint stuck in the way, keeping the dryer from doing what it was created to do. My heart desires to be pure of regret, sinful thoughts, old thinking, disturbing words from others that get stuck, and so many other distractions that keep me from doing what I was made to do. Heal me, Jesus! Cleanse my heart of the old junk. Purify my heart so that I can be set free from the past pain! I love you, Jesus! Thank you, Jesus! Amen!"

Day 3
Jesus Sees Your Faith

A few days later, when Jesus again entered Capernaum, the people heard that he had come home. They gathered in such large numbers that there was no room left, not even outside the door, and he preached the word to them. Some men came, bringing to him a paralyzed man, carried by four of them. Since they could not get him to Jesus because of the crowd, they made an opening in the roof above Jesus by digging through it and then lowered the mat the man was lying on. When Jesus saw their faith, he said to the paralyzed man, "Son, your sins are forgiven."
--Mark 2: 1-5

Imagine that you were at the church gathering in Capernaum that day, listening to Jesus preach. Try to imagine what it would be like when, all of a sudden, the roof of the place starts falling down on you and the people around you! You'd wonder what was happening, right? And then, you look up to see the guy on a mat, lowered down through the hole in the ceiling. That had to be quite a sight to see!

I would be focused on the paralyzed man – the center of attention for this show. But that's where I again differ from Jesus. He focused on the four men carrying him – the friends of the paralyzed man. Amazing! He was not distracted from the ceiling falling down, the interruptions in the middle of his sermon, the disruptions and the noises of the crowd – nope.

His focus was on the faith of the four men, who believed so strongly that Jesus could heal their friend. Jesus simply proclaimed a miracle: "Son, your sins are forgiven."

Isn't it AMAZING how Jesus responds?
He sees our faith. And it matters to Him.

* * *

BE STRONG!

1. When Jesus looks at <u>your</u> faith, what does He see?

   a. Is Jesus pleased with your faith?

   b. Is Jesus not pleased with your faith?

2. Intimacy with Christ sustains my intensity and impact for the kingdom of heaven here on earth. How can we gain more faith in Jesus Christ?

   a. Jesus answered, "It is written: 'Man shall not live on bread alone, but on every word that comes from the mouth of God'" (Matthew 4:4).

      How many times per day do you feed your physical body? You probably eat three, four, five or more times per day, right? Scripture tells us that man cannot live on bread alone, but also by the word of God. So, if you are only taking in God's word once per day, it's like you're on a fast. Doesn't it make sense to "eat and drink" of His word three, four, or five or more times per day? Give your body, mind, and soul the sustenance they need.

   b. "Consequently, faith comes from hearing the message, and the message is heard through the word about Christ" (Romans 10:17).

      Listen to Bible teachers at your church and/or online. Faith comes from hearing the Word of God.

c. Pray continually (1 Thessalonians 5:17).

Talk to JESUS! Jesus desires to spend time with YOU. Bring your requests before the Lord in prayer. Ask Him for more faith in Jesus.

PRAYER

Lord, we are HUNGRY for MORE of YOU!
Give us a deeper desire to crave your Words of life and fill us until we overflow. We want MORE faith. More of YOU, Jesus! Amen.

Day 4
Be a God Pleaser
(Not a Friend Pleaser)

Am I now trying to win the approval of human beings, or of God?
Or am I trying to please people? If I were still trying to please people, I
would not be a servant of Christ. --Galatians 1:10

"As for other matters, brothers and sisters, **we instructed you how to**
live in order to please God, *as in fact you are living. Now we ask*
you and urge you in the Lord Jesus to do this more and more. For you know
what instructions we gave you by the authority of the Lord Jesus. It is God's
will that you should be sanctified: that you should avoid sexual immorality;
that each of you should learn to control your own body in a way that is holy
and honorable, not in passionate lust like the pagans, who do not know
God; and that in this matter no one should wrong or take advantage of a
brother or sister. The Lord will punish all those who commit such sins, as
we told you and warned you before. For God did not call us to be impure,
but to live a holy life. **Therefore, anyone who rejects this**
instruction does not reject a human being but God, the very
God who gives you his Holy Spirit. *Now about your love for one*
another we do not need to write to you, for you yourselves have been taught by
God to love each other. And in fact, you do love all of God's family
throughout Macedonia. Yet we urge you, brothers and sisters, to do so more
and more, and to make it your ambition to lead a quiet life: You should
mind your own business and work with your hands, just as we told you, so
that your daily life may win the respect of outsiders and so that you will not
be dependent on anybody." --1 Thessalonians 4:1-12

Too often in my life, I find myself wanting the approval of my
friends, family, neighbors, coworkers, customers, strangers, and
many others. Why?

The basic answer is simple: I want to be liked and loved by
others. So, I please them by giving them what they want. I may do
this by listening to an off-color joke, talking about someone
behind his or her back, being overly critical of a pastor, preacher,
or Christians who attend a church that is different from my own.

Unfortunately, this type of people-pleasing isn't aligned with God's will.

*   *   *

BE STRONG!

1. Nobody on the planet knows you better than you know yourself. So, be honest with yourself in this moment. Are you a God pleaser or a man pleaser? Can you sense, at times, that you find yourself doing things that are not "the best," just to appease others so that you can be liked or not be disruptive?

2. What causes you to need the affirmations and acceptance of others, even those who may not play central, important roles in your life?

3. Be a God pleaser. What do you need to stop doing today so that you can become more like Jesus and less like your broken self?
    As Paul wrote:
    For God did not call us to be impure, but to live a holy life. (1 Thessalonians 4:7)

PRAYER

Oh God, forgive me for focusing too much on what others think or say about me. At times, I have made them too important. Help me, to keep the main thing, the main thing. God you are the main thing in my life.
Jesus, I want to be a God pleaser, not a man pleaser.
Thank you, for hearing and answering my prayer for help! Amen.

Day 5
Hardships
(Be Encouraged)

"For my thoughts are not your thoughts, neither are your ways my ways,"
declares the Lord. --Isaiah 55:8

Life is not easy. In fact, life is tough. Are you in a tough situation that you are not enjoying? You're in good company!

When God came to earth as a man, Jesus took on all of life's situations. Life for Jesus was tough. He faced everything any other man would face—except that He never sinned. Jesus endured the hardships and tough situations. I trust that He did not like everything, but He endured.

- **Endurance**: the fact or power of enduring an unpleasant or difficult process or situation without giving way.

When you are in a "tough situation" that calls for endurance, where do you focus your attention? Where does your mind go? Does it try to immediately fix it? Do you find yourself focused on how to move from tough to easy, how to resolve the discomfort?

Therefore, since we are surrounded by such a great cloud of witnesses, let us throw off everything that hinders and the sin that so easily entangles. And let us run with perseverance the race marked out for us, fixing our eyes on Jesus, the pioneer and perfecter of faith. For the joy set before him he endured the cross, scorning its shame, and sat down at the right hand of the throne of God. Consider him who endured such opposition from sinners, so that you will not grow weary and lose heart. (Hebrews 12:1-3)

What is the writer of Hebrews trying to tell us when he encourages us to *fix our eyes on Jesus*?

Would you consider that God's ways are not your ways? Perhaps, in His amazing love, He is trying to teach you something from and through the hardship.

"For my thoughts are not your thoughts, neither are your ways my ways,"
declares the Lord.
(Isaiah 55:8)

* * *

BE STRONG!

1. Pain can be a great teacher, especially for men who are strong-minded, headstrong, thick-headed, know-it-all perfectionists. You know who I'm talking about! Is that you?

2. Read these words:

   Not only so, but we also glory in our sufferings, because we know that suffering produces perseverance; perseverance, character; and character, hope. And hope does not put us to shame, because God's love has been poured out into our hearts through the Holy Spirit, who has been given to us. Romans 5: 3-5

   What might God be trying to tell you about the presence of hardships and pain in your life?

3. Pray. Ask the Lord to speak to your heart about hardship and pain you are experiencing. Ask Him, "Jesus, what are you trying to teach me?"

4. WRITE down what the Lord has spoken or shown to you today.

PRAYER

Jesus, I don't like pain. The truth is, I like pleasure. I know that pain can be a great attention-getting tool to wake-me UP from my slumber. I ask that I can learn and grow in character from the painful situations in my life. I want to grow and mature to be MORE LIKE YOU, JESUS! Amen.

Day 6
What Did You Lose?

Every good and perfect gift is from the above.
--James 1:17

Have you ever thought about how much you have? Today, I challenge you to do an inventory of what you have been given as a gift from our Lord! It's easy to do, and a good reminder of the numerous blessings that have been entrusted to you – from our Father in Heaven!

Here is the beginning of my list:

- I can see (eyesight).
- I can read (literacy)!
- I have fingers that allow me to turn the pages of this book.
- I have clean clothes to wear, and I have an additional inventory of clothing for many days to come.
- I have plenty of food and drink. And maybe I have extra food in the pantry, freezer and refrigerator.
- I have money.
- I have a job and the ability to work.
- I have a place to sleep.
- I can make friends.
- I have people in my life who know me, like me, and love me.
- I have salvation and faith in the risen Christ!
- I have access to a church that enables me to gather with others and worship our Lord.

- I have a Father in Heaven, a friend in Jesus, and the power of the Holy Spirit deposited in my heart! WOW!

(... Keep going...)

Now, look back over the course of your life, and identify what you have lost over the years.

What have you lost?

1. Have you lost friends?
2. Have you lost relationships with people who matter to you (family, co-workers, church, etc.)?
3. Have you lost your health?
4. Have you lost your job?
5. Have you lost your financial wealth?
6. Have you lost your home?
7. Have you lost touch with people who know you, like you, and love you?
8. Have you lost your parents? Children? Grandparents? Sister and/or brothers?
9. Have you lost your true self due to drifting too far from the truth and the Word of God?
10. Have you lost your faith in the God of miracles, the Resurrection and the Life, the Bread of Life, the Way, the Truth and the Life?

What have you lost? Everyone who has lived has experienced loss.

WRITE it down.

* * *

BE STRONG!

1. Pray. Let's simply begin by giving thanks to the Giver of good gifts. Say, "Thank you, Jesus! Thank you,

Father! Thank you, Holy Spirit for all the blessings in my life!"

PRAYER

"Jesus, as I begin to remember and confess my losses to you, it can feel like a hole in my heart that needs to be filled. Lord, I ask You to fill that hole with more of you. I long for your love, grace, holiness, comfort, and the peace that only comes from you. Amen.

But whatever were gains to me I now consider loss for the sake of Christ. What is more, I consider everything a loss because of the surpassing worth of knowing Christ Jesus my Lord, for whose sake I have lost all things. I consider them garbage, that I may gain Christ.
(Philippians 3:7-8)

Day 7
4th Quarter

Our days may come to seventy years,
or eighty, if our strength endures;
yet the best of them are but trouble and sorrow,
for they quickly pass, and we fly away.
--Psalm 90:10

I like football!

I was blessed to play for nine years through high school and college. I recall a football coach telling the team, "Life is like a football game." As I've gotten older, I realize that he was right. There are many parallels between football and living a Christ-centered life.

How so?

1. Everyone is given a fixed amount of time. You must maximize the amount of time that is on the clock.
2. Each member of the team is given a role or a position (a unique calling, life mission and/or talent).
3. Each player is trained or encouraged to give his very best effort for his individual role. By doing so, each player will do well, and the team will do well.
4. Each season is different, due to the unpredictability of the ever-changing environment (team members, opposition, weather, travel, equipment, injuries, off-the-field influences, etc.).

5. You must be strong to be a good football player. You cannot gain strength while just playing football. You must get off the field and train hard in the strength room with weight training. This extra effort off the field will benefit you greatly for your role on the team.

6. You must be humble or coachable in order to grow and become the best that you can be – successful on and off the field. Distractions like pride, arrogance, or the selfishness of an individual will lead to defeat.

7. The average team executes 75 offensive and defensive plays per game. Similarly, the average lifespan of an American male is 76.4 years.

8. Each play builds upon the other, and not every play is designed to score a touchdown. Trust that each play (or day in life) builds towards the end zone.

*　*　*

BE STRONG!

1. Pause for a moment and consider your age. What quarter of life are you in, currently?
   a. 1st Quarter: age 0-20 years old
   b. 2nd Quarter: age 21-40 years old
   c. 3rd Quarter: age 41-60 years old
   d. 4th Quarter: age 61-80 years old
   e. Overtime: 81 years old or more

2. Now, make a list of your roles and positions:
   a. Marriage (Husband)

      b.   Worker

      c.   Father

      d.   Ministry

      e.   Brother

      f.   Son

      g.   Grandfather

      h.   Friend

      i.   Church _____

      j.   Other: _____

      k. _____

      l. _____

3.   Only so much time is left on the clock for your life. Pray and ask our Lord to help you prioritize which roles require the greatest investment of the fixed amount of time remaining.

      a.   My three MOST important roles in this quarter of my life:

          i. _____

          ii. _____

          iii. _____

4.   What heart thoughts need to be written down and prayed over as you seek to know God's "game plan" for you during this quarter of your life?

*For I know the plans I have for you," declares the Lord, "plans to prosper
you and not to harm you, plans to give you hope and a future.
(Jeremiah 29:11)*

PRAYER

*Jesus, we know that time is running out. I'm in the ____ quarter of my life
and I only have some many days remaining. I ask that you direct my steps,
my actions, my priorities to align with YOUR WILL. May your will be
done in my life so that I can finish STRONG, for YOU! Amen.*

Day 8
Let's Pray Together!

The prayer of a righteous man is powerful and effective. --James 5:16

Did you know that the Bible contains examples of prayer teams? Check out the story of Moses' prayer team:

As long as Moses held up his hands, the Israelites were winning, but whenever he lowered his hands, the Amalekites were winning. When Moses' hands grew tired, they took a stone and put it under him and he sat on it. Aaron and Hur held his hands up—one on one side, one on the other—so that his hands remained steady till sunset. So Joshua overcame the Amalekite army with the sword.
--Exodus 17:11-13

Look at the story of Peter's prayer team:
So Peter was kept in prison, but the church was earnestly praying to God for him.

The night before Herod was to bring him to trial, Peter was sleeping between two soldiers, bound with two chains, and sentries stood guard at the entrance. Suddenly an angel of the Lord appeared and a light shone in the cell. He struck Peter on the side and woke him up. "Quick, get up!" he said, and the chains fell off Peter's wrists.

Then the angel said to him, "Put on your clothes and sandals." And Peter did so. "Wrap your cloak around you and follow me," the angel told him. Peter followed him out of the prison, but he had no idea that what the angel was doing was really happening; he thought he was seeing a vision. They passed the first and second guards and came to the iron gate leading to the city. It opened for them by itself, and they went through it. When they had walked the length of one street, suddenly the angel left him.

Then Peter came to himself and said, "Now I know without a doubt that the Lord has sent his angel and rescued me from Herod's clutches and from everything the Jewish people were hoping would happen."

When this had dawned on him, he went to the house of Mary the mother of John, also called Mark, where many people had gathered and were praying. (Acts 12:5-12)

Amazing feats can happen when God's people get together and pray! We need to pray that more people will draw closer to Jesus. He longs to draw closer to us!

"Submit yourselves, then, to God. Resist the devil, and he will flee from you. Come near to God and he will come near to you. Wash your hands, you sinners, and purify your hearts, you double-minded." *(James 4:7-8)*

* * *

BE STRONG!

1. Do you pray regularly throughout your day?

2. Do you ask others to pray for you?
   a. If the answer is yes, well done! Your humility is a strength.

   b. If you do not, what keeps you from opening your heart and asking for help? If Jesus had others praying for Him, don't you think that you should too?

3. Let's pray. James suggests that we submit to God as our first step. What can you lay down in submission to our Lord today?

   a. Worry

   b. Control

   c. Your will

d. _____ {fill in}

4. James then suggests that we resist Satan. Do you stand up against his evil influence on you? What do you need to resist in your life today that is coming from the pit of hell?

   a. Temptation

   b. Lust

   c. Selfishness

   d. Greed

   e. _____ {fill in}

5. Lastly, James directs us to take action. He tells us to move, or to "draw near to God, and God will draw near to you." James' instructions imply that you need to make the first move. What are you going to do?

PRAYER

God you are awesome! Thank you for wanting to draw closer to me! I want to draw closer to you, Lord! I submit my will and desire to do your will today, Jesus. I resist the enemy's attempt to block or influence me and my decisions. I open myself to hear from Heaven and ask for the faith to execute with excellence! I pray this in the mighty name of JESUS my Lord and my God! Amen

Day 9
Are You a Follower?

For my Father's will is that everyone who looks to the Son and believes in him shall have eternal life, and I will raise them up at the last day."
--John 6:40

For whoever does the will of my Father in heaven is my brother and sister and mother.
--Matthew 12:50

Are you a follower?

This question is not so popular, is it? Most men and women want to be leaders, not followers. Have you ever considered that Jesus was both? Jesus was a great leader and a great follower. It is obvious that he was a great leader, since you and I have chosen to follow Him. But he was a great follower of His Father's will. WOW!

How can we learn to follow our Father's will? Let's look to Jesus and learn what He did.

First of all, **He *humbled* Himself.** He did not do His will, but instead Jesus humbled Himself to do the will of His Father. He followed His Father's will.

> *6 Who, being in very nature God,*
> *did not consider equality with God something to be used to his own advantage;*
> *7 rather, he made himself nothing*
> *by taking the very nature of a servant,*
> *being made in human likeness.*
> *8 And being found in appearance as a man,*
> *he humbled himself*
> *by becoming obedient to death—*
> *even death on a cross!*
> *9 Therefore God exalted him to the highest place*
> *and gave him the name that is above every name,*

10 that at the name of Jesus every knee should bow,
   in heaven and on earth and under the earth,
11 and every tongue acknowledge that Jesus Christ is Lord,
   to the glory of God the Father.
(Philippians 2:6-11)

HOW do we do that?

"Jesus called the crowd together with His disciples, and said to them, "If anyone wishes to follow Me [as My disciple], he must deny himself [set aside selfish interests], and take up his cross [expressing a willingness to endure whatever may come] and follow Me [believing in Me, conforming to My example in living and, if need be, suffering or perhaps dying because of faith in Me]." (Mark 8:34) (AMP)

* * *

BE STRONG!

1. Are you humble enough <u>to be a FOLLOWER</u> of God's will for your life?

2. What do you <u>need to surrender</u> today in order to be a GREAT follower of Jesus?

   a. What part of your ego needs to be submitted?

   b. Hold your wallet in your hand. What finances need to be surrendered to God?

c. What about your physical health? What concerns need to be submitted?

d. What are your "legalistic views" of Christianity? What man-made rules need to be laid down at the cross of Christ?

e. What about your job? Is it an idol compared to your worship of our Lord? What part of your career, job, employment needs to be submissive to God's will?

3. What prayer do you need to lift up to Heaven as you commit to being a follower of our Father's will for your life?

PRAYER

Jesus, I confess that too often I resist following your lead. It is not good. I laydown every distraction that kicks me off of the path that you have laid out for my life. Help me! I want to be a great follower of your leadership, Lord! Amen.

Day 10
Faith Moves Mountains

Truly I tell you, if you have faith as small as a mustard seed, you can say to this mountain, 'Move from here to there,' and it will move. Nothing will be impossible for you. --Matthew 17:20

Faith moves mountains because our God doesn't see the problem as a mountain. He sees miniature molehills!

I'm referencing the God of Heaven and earth. He is the Creator, the Alpha and the Omega. Big obstacles in our human life are tiny in His eyes. Of course, to us, each problem is a BIG, BIG deal that causes us to feel fear, doubt, anxiety, and other distracting emotions.

The power of your faith is directly proportional to the size of the one in whom you have that faith. It's not about the size of your faith, but the one in whom you have placed your faith. (Read it again).

So, the question is this:
How BIG is your JESUS?
Who is Jesus to you?
Is He the GOD of miracles and the One who promises new LIFE?

~ ~ ~

Jesus, defeated death – when **He rose from the grave** after being crucified.

Jesus Has Risen
28 After the Sabbath, at dawn on the first day of the week, Mary Magdalene and the other Mary went to look at the tomb.
2 There was a violent earthquake, for an angel of the Lord came down from heaven and, going to the tomb, rolled back the stone and sat on it. 3 His appearance was like lightning, and his clothes were white as snow. 4 The guards were so afraid of him that they shook and became like dead men.

5 The angel said to the women, "Do not be afraid, for I know that you are looking for Jesus, who was crucified. 6 He is not here; he has risen, just as he said. Come and see the place where he lay. 7 Then go quickly and tell his disciples: 'He has risen from the dead and is going ahead of you into Galilee. There you will see him.' Now I have told you."

8 So the women hurried away from the tomb, afraid yet filled with joy, and ran to tell his disciples. 9 Suddenly Jesus met them. "Greetings," he said. They came to him, clasped his feet and worshiped him. 10 Then Jesus said to them, "Do not be afraid. Go and tell my brothers to go to Galilee; there they will see me."
(Matthew 28:1-10)

~ ~ ~

Jesus, defeated death – when He told Lazarus to come out of the tomb.

Jesus Raises Lazarus From the Dead

38 Jesus, once more deeply moved, came to the tomb. It was a cave with a stone laid across the entrance. 39 "Take away the stone," he said.

"But, Lord," said Martha, the sister of the dead man, "by this time there is a bad odor, for he has been there four days."

40 Then Jesus said, "Did I not tell you that if you believe, you will see the glory of God?"

41 So they took away the stone. Then Jesus looked up and said, "Father, I thank you that you have heard me. 42 I knew that you always hear me, but I said this for the benefit of the people standing here, that they may believe that you sent me."

43 When he had said this, Jesus called in a loud voice, "Lazarus, come out!" 44 The dead man came out, his hands and feet wrapped with strips of linen, and a cloth around his face.

Jesus said to them, "Take off the grave clothes and let him go."
(John 11:38-44)

~ ~ ~

Jesus, defeated death – when He brought the dead child back to life and gave him back to his mother.

Jesus Raises a Widow's Son

11 Soon afterward, Jesus went to a town called Nain, and his disciples and a large crowd went along with him. 12 As he approached the town gate, a dead person was being carried out—the only son of his mother, and she was a widow. And a large crowd from the town was with her. 13 When the Lord saw her, his heart went out to her and he said, "Don't cry."

14 Then he went up and touched the bier they were carrying him on, and the bearers stood still. He said, "Young man, I say to you, get up!" 15 The dead man sat up and began to talk, and Jesus gave him back to his mother.

16 They were all filled with awe and praised God. "A great prophet has appeared among us," they said. "God has come to help his people." 17 This news about Jesus spread throughout Judea and the surrounding country.

(Luke 7:11-17)

~ ~ ~

Jesus defeated all kinds of illnesses.

Jesus Heals

38 Jesus left the synagogue and went to the home of Simon. Now Simon's mother-in-law was suffering from a high fever, and they asked Jesus to help her. 39 So he bent over her and rebuked the fever, and it left her. She got up at once and began to wait on them.
(Luke 4:38-39)

How deep is your faith in the One who can perform these miracles?

* * *

BE STRONG!

1. What can keep you from having great faith? Look at this list. Write down your truth.

- Doubt. What do you doubt?

- Lies. What lies do you tell yourself?

- Lack of trust. Who do you NOT trust?

- Past experiences: What happened in the past that caused your faith to become smaller or ineffective?

- Fear: List 3 of your greatest fears:

    1.

    2.

    3.

2. You and I get to make a choice every day, whether to live in fear or to live in faith. God hasn't given us fear, but the Enemy tries to make us fall into his trap of lies. Knowing this, will you choose fear or faith?

    "For the Spirit God gave us does not make us timid, but gives us power, love and self-discipline." (2 Timothy 1:7)

"The Spirit you received does not make you slaves, so that you live in fear again; rather, the Spirit you received brought about your adoption to sonship. And by him we cry, "Abba, Father." " (Romans 8:15)

3. Jesus knows that we need more faith. Ask Him to give you the faith you need.

He replied, "Because you have so little faith. Truly I tell you, if you have faith as small as a mustard seed, you can say to this mountain, 'Move from here to there,' and it will move. Nothing will be impossible for you." (Matthew 17:20)

PRAYER

GREAT FAITH is what I desire, Lord. Help me to know you MORE so that that my faith may grow. I want Holy Spirit power to grow my faith! Let the power of my faith be directly proportional to the size of the one in whom I have faith. God that would be awesome! Thank you, JESUS! Amen.

Day 11
Who am I?

For you created my inmost being;
you knit me together in my mother's womb.
--Psalm 139:13

God determined your gender. God had a purpose for you when He created you as a man.

Consider these four truths:

1.   God created gender, and He loves both genders.

> *"So God created mankind in his own image, in the image of God he created them; male and female he created them." (Genesis 1:27)*

2.   God decided your gender.

> *13 For you created my inmost being;*
> *you knit me together in my mother's womb.*
> *14 I praise you because I am fearfully and wonderfully made;*
> *your works are wonderful,*
> *I know that full well.*
> *15 My frame was not hidden from you*
> *when I was made in the secret place,*
> *when I was woven together in the depths of the earth.*
> *16 Your eyes saw my unformed body;*
> *all the days ordained for me were written in your book*
> *before one of them came to be. (Psalm 139:13-16)*

3.   God has established our gender relationship as one of interdependence. He has established a divine order (kingdom authority) based on gender, and these roles depend on one another. Clearly, it is easy to see this interdependence in procreation.

10 It is for this reason that a woman ought to have authority over her own head, because of the angels. 11 Nevertheless, in the Lord woman is not independent of man, nor is man independent of woman. 12 For as woman came from man, so also man is born of woman. But everything comes from God. (1 Corinthians 11:10-12)

4.   God has given you authority and purpose. Our human authority is in Christ, and He has equipped us and sends us with purpose and mission.

18 Then Jesus came to them and said, "All authority in heaven and on earth has been given to me. 19 Therefore go and make disciples of all nations, baptizing them in the name of the Father and of the Son and of the Holy Spirit, 20 and teaching them to obey everything I have commanded you. And surely I am with you always, to the very end of the age." (Matthew 28:18-20)

*   *   *

BE STRONG!

1.   I need to know WHO I am. If I had male genitalia when I was born, then obviously I was created to be a man, and this is good. Do you enjoy how God created you? List three things that you enjoy about being a man:

    a.

    b.

    c.

2.   I find it both humbling and exciting that we as men are in an interdependent relationship with women! It is humbling to know I need help, that I need others in my

life. The opposite gender brings unique and awesome gifts to the relationship. It is exciting because it is fun and enjoyable to experience a loving relationship with the opposite gender!

He answered, "Have you not read that he who created them from the beginning made them male and female, and said, 'Therefore a man shall leave his father and his mother and hold fast to his wife, and the two shall become one flesh'? So they are no longer two but one flesh. What therefore God has joined together, let not man separate." (Matthew 19:4-6) (ESV)

Therefore a man shall leave his father and mother and hold fast to his wife, and the two shall become one flesh. (Ephesians 5:31) (ESV)

PRAYER

Jesus, thank you for making me a man. Help me fulfill my role as a man whom You have created. Help me to honor women with great respect and honor today. Amen.

Day 12
Why Do I Have Enemies?

"You have heard that it was said, 'Love your neighbor and hate your enemy.' But I tell you, love your enemies and pray for those who persecute you...
--Matthew 5:43-44

When I Google the word *enemy*, I find this definition: a person who is actively opposed or hostile to someone or something.

Think about your life. Has anyone ever opposed your idea, your way of thinking, how you live, your faith, or something you said? Your answer is "yes." Of course, it is! God knew that you would experience some friction or resistance from others. It is not a surprise.

What may be a surprise is that all too often we have active opposition or friction from friends, family and other Christians. Ugh—that's a harder reality to face.

Jesus said, "Love your enemies,"

> *43 "You have heard that it was said, 'Love your neighbor and hate your enemy.' 44 But I tell you, love your enemies and pray for those who persecute you, 45 that you may be children of your Father in heaven. He causes his sun to rise on the evil and the good, and sends rain on the righteous and the unrighteous. 46 If you love those who love you, what reward will you get? Are not even the tax collectors doing that? 47 And if you greet only your own people, what are you doing more than others? Do not even pagans do that? 48 Be perfect, therefore, as your heavenly Father is perfect. (Matthew 5:43-48)*

God knew that we would have enemies. Unfortunately, even within our churches we can persecute one another. Why?

There can be a host of reasons, including polarizing theological issues, past experiences, unstated expectations, conversations that were misunderstood, envy, jealousy or simply that your enemy may not like you.

It is possible that the friction is not even about you; rather, the other person may be dealing with something deeply rooted in them. Maybe they are angry with God. They just take it out on you, maybe without even knowing it.

The bottom line is this: God is in charge. He allows us to have enemies. This fits His purposes to raise us up or mature us. For reasons only God knows, this is what we need. It helps to humble us. An enemy can be like a mirror, showing us what we are like. The next time you feel tension with an enemy, try this: don't be angry with your enemy. Instead, consider that it is God who is at work on your heart to make you STRONGER.

*   *   *

BE STRONG!

Grow STRONGER! Paul wrote:

That is why, for Christ's sake, I delight in weaknesses, in insults, in hardships, in persecutions, in difficulties. For when I am weak, then I am strong. (2 Corinthians 12:10)

1. Do you have an enemy in your life now? Someone who is causing you friction? Good! God is working on your heart to make you stronger and more Christ-like. Thank the Lord for seeing weakness in you that He can make strong.

2. Humble yourself as you hold up the mirror. Ask God to take away any part of your character that is similar to what you dislike most about your enemy or your opposition.

3. "Peace. Peace be with you." Imagine saying that to your enemy. Wow. Quite possibly, God is asking you to have a peaceful heart towards your enemy. You can begin to

love your enemies by praying for them, asking the Lord to give them peace.

PRAYER

Jesus, your love for me and your enemies is mind-blowing. How do you do it? Help me to have a heart of love like yours. I ask that you bless my enemy. (Name the person before the Lord.) May I have peace in my heart that comes from the Holy Spirit. Thank you, Lord! Amen.

Day 13
Who Is Wise?

13 Who is wise and understanding among you? Let them show it by their good life, by deeds done in the humility that comes from wisdom. 14 But if you harbor bitter envy and selfish ambition in your hearts, do not boast about it or deny the truth. 15 Such "wisdom" does not come down from heaven but is earthly, unspiritual, demonic. 16 For where you have envy and selfish ambition, there you find disorder and every evil practice.
17 But the wisdom that comes from heaven is first of all pure; then peace-loving, considerate, submissive, full of mercy and good fruit, impartial and sincere.
--James 3:13-17

Do you consider yourself to have WISDOM from heaven? I hope so!

Test yourself, as James points out in verse 13 (above). Does your life demonstrate God's goodness through actions taken in humility? Or are you primarily demonstrating how good you are, and then proclaiming it to everyone that will listen?

Filter your actions and decisions through the list in verse 17. Seek that your decisions are pure, peace loving, considerate, submissive, full of mercy and good fruit, impartial and sincere.

* * *

BE STRONG!

If you were asked for advice or wisdom to share with others, what would you say? Would your words be God-centered or something-else-centered?

Throughout my years as a believer, I have gathered a collection of Wisdom Statements. Here is my list:

Be Strong!

Top Seven Wisdom Statements from Spice

1. Make God the most important part of your life. Everything else is secondary. Consume His Word (Bible) throughout each day. Talk to Him. He hears you and will answer your prayers!

2. Make your wife the most important human in your life. Prove it to her every day.

3. Be an encourager of others, and you too will be encouraged.

4. The best prayer you can ask: "Jesus, what do YOU want me to do?" And then listen. Then do #5.

5. Give your very best effort in all that you do. Jesus gave 100%. How much are you giving?

6. Creativity is endless. Look up and see God's endless creativity.

7. Your breaths are numbered. As you take another one, that is minus one from all you have remaining. Make them count – let's GO!

Now you try it. What are your top 7 wisdom statements? Pray first and ask God to guide you in this exercise.

"JESUS, I know that wisdom comes from Heaven. So, I ask that you fill my mind and heart thoughts with Your thoughts. Help me to be wise. Amen!"

Top Seven Wisdom Statements from

_____

(Your Name)

    1.

    2.

    3.

    4.

    5.

    6.

    7.

PRAYER

Wisdom is precious to me. Lord, I ask that I can grow in the wisdom from Heaven that is; pure, peace loving, considerate, submissive, full of mercy and good fruit, impartial and sincere. Amen.

Day 14
WORK OUT?

*24 Do you not know that in a race all the runners run, but only one gets the prize? Run in such a way as to get the prize. 25 Everyone who competes in the games goes into strict training. They do it to get a crown that will not last, **but we do it to get a crown that will last forever.**
26 Therefore I do not run like someone running aimlessly; I do not fight like a boxer beating the air.
27 No, I strike a blow to my body and make it my slave so that after I have preached to others, I myself will not be disqualified for the prize.
--1 Corinthians 9:24-27*

Do you work out? Are you regularly training your body though diet and exercise so that you can be healthy and strong? I hope so!

Let's dig in to both elements of building a healthy and strong physical body: Diet and Exercise.

1. **DIET:** How many times today will you feed your body? Many health experts advise us to eat multiple smaller meals throughout the day, rather than two or three large meals. This healthy practice is to maintain our weight, aid in digestion, and avoid overeating. How are you doing in eating both in frequency and in quantity?

2. **EXERCISE:** By now, we have heard it over and over: we should exercise our bodies three to five times per week, each time for twenty minutes or more. This includes lifting weights and cardiovascular conditioning. The intensity of our exercise should increase our muscle strength and our heart health. How are you doing?

8 For physical training is of some value, but godliness has value for all things, holding promise for both the present life and the life to come. 9 This is a trustworthy saying that deserves full acceptance. 10 That is why we labor and strive, because we have put our hope in the living God, who is the Savior of all people, and especially of those who believe. (1 Timothy 4:8-10)

Paul wrote these words in each of these letters. Clearly, Paul was focused, self-disciplined, and of high intensity! I love it!

How about you? Do you live your life to "give your very best" to WIN the RACE? Do you train your inner man, your core self, and your soul to grow in Christ? How?

DIET: How many times today will you feed your soul? God's WORD is life! We need to eat it, consume it, take-it-in from the start of the day to the end. If I eat five physical meals per day, shouldn't I eat at least five meals of God's WORD every day?

EXERCISE: If all I do is to go to church once a week, that is NOT much of a soul workout is it? So, if I want to train and be **strong** in my faith, I need to work out every day! This includes a steady **daily** regime of prayer, worship and Scripture.

* * *

BE STRONG!

1. You and I need a daily regimen of time with God, and we can build this in multiple ways:

    a. **Prayer:** I need to talk to Jesus regularly throughout each day!

        Pray continually. (1 Thessalonians 5:17)

    b. **Worship**: Praise Him. Thank Him. Love Him with your words and actions.
        God is spirit, and his worshipers must worship in the Spirit and in truth. (John 4:24)

    c. **Scripture**: Read God's word and live a life that is full and abundant.

        Very truly I tell you, whoever hears my word and believes him who sent me has eternal life and will not be judged but has crossed over from death to life. (John 5:24)

The Spirit gives life; the flesh counts for nothing. The words I have spoken to you—they are full of the Spirit and life. (John 6:63)

Simon Peter answered him, "Lord, to whom shall we go? You have the words of eternal life." (John 6:68)

PRAYER

"God, I want to be STRONG for You! I ask for the gift of self-discipline so that I can train up both my body and soul with a daily regimen of physical work and soul work. I want to have less of me and more of you! Amen."

Day 15
Life is a Journey

"And we all, who with unveiled faces contemplate the Lord's glory, are being transformed into his image with ever-increasing glory, which comes from the Lord, who is the Spirit." --2 Corinthians 3:18

Life is a process as we move through various stages, from infant to elder.

Life is about character, not accomplishments. Accomplishments fade, but character does not. It is about who we are, not *what* we do. What we can do today will not always be available in the future. Who I am remains throughout life.

Life is about trust. It is not about control. We live by faith and not by sight. (2 Corinthians 5:7)

Life usually involves a crisis, a great pain. Life involves our greatest fears and our greatest failures. Pain is a great teacher in our lives.

These transformation moments can lead us to maturity in Christ.

At key points in the journey, we need other people. Community is the essence of our triune God!

May the grace of the Lord Jesus Christ, and the love of God, and the fellowship of the Holy Spirit be with you all. (2 Corinthians 13:14)

COMPONENTS to JOURNEY WELL

> **Community** comes from being in relationships with others and in relationship with Christ. I decide to relate or not with others (with God). It is an every-day process, multiple times per day.

> **Journey** is moving forward. I must decide to move or act. It is my choice. Sedentary lifestyle leads to disease and disability. I want a full life and to live with ZEAL!

Never be lacking in zeal, but keep your spiritual fervor, serving the Lord. Romans 12:11

➤ **Change or Transformation** starts with me. It is an inside-out process of digging in and getting out. Radical transformation of our character is rooted in God's amazing love. **HE** wants us to grow up and mature, **to be MORE LIKE JESUS!**

Character change...

"Not only so, but we also glory in our sufferings, because we know that suffering produces perseverance; perseverance, character; and character, hope. And hope does not put us to shame, because God's love has been poured out into our hearts through the Holy Spirit, who has been given to us." (Romans 5:3-5)

"Consider it pure joy, my brothers and sisters, whenever you face trials of many kinds, because you know that the testing of your faith produces perseverance. Let perseverance finish its work so that you may be mature and complete, not lacking anything." (James 1:2-4)

*   *   *

BE STRONG!

1. <u>Rate</u> the following five elements on a scale of 1 to 10 (10 is High) as they exist in your life today.

- **Honesty**: when we tell <u>others</u> the truth.
- **Integrity**: when we tell <u>ourselves</u> the truth.
- **Confession**: when we tell <u>GOD</u> the truth. The words coming out of my mouth, God would agree are true and accurate.

- **Trust**: when I can be confident in "you" even when I cannot see you.
- **Safety**: when I can "be the real me" (emotional and physical) in front of others (and GOD).

2. What do you want to do, now that you have completed Step 1? Write your response:

PRAYER

"Jesus, Your life on earth was an amazing journey! We need ALL of You on our life journey. Through YOU, we grow, mature, and receive NEW LIFE, every day with every breath! THANK YOU, LORD! We ask for Your amazing grace, love, and fellowship until our last breath on earth. Amen!"

May the grace of the Lord Jesus Christ, and the love of God, and the fellowship of the Holy Spirit be with you all.
(2 Corinthians 13:14)

Day 16
Grace

For it is by grace you have been saved, through faith—and this is not from yourselves, it is the gift of God—not by works, so that no one can boast.
--Ephesians 2:8-9

Grace can be defined as "the unmerited favor of God toward man." Jesus is a model of God's grace to us, so we can best understand by understanding Jesus Christ.

Have you ever read the last verse in your Bible? Check it out: *The grace of the Lord Jesus be with God's people. Amen. (Revelation 22:21)*

Wow! That's *amazing* that the Bible ends with three key elements:

1. Grace
2. Jesus our Lord
3. Mankind (God's people)

God's love for his people is unmerited, which means it is not earned or deserved. God's favor and His acts of kindness are beyond anything normal, expected, or due. This is mind blowing! We are not saved by our good deeds or moral living. We are saved by only trusting in Jesus Christ. This is the gift of love from God. This is God's miracle!

You see, God initiated loving us. He is the one who started the "I love you" communication. When someone in your life says, "I love you," what is your typical verbal response? Of course, it is "I love you, too!"

With every sunrise, every new morning of new mercies, God is telling us that He loves us. Our response is, "I love you, too!"

* * *

BE STRONG!

1. Read these words from John.

7 Dear friends, let us love one another, for love comes from God. Everyone who loves has been born of God and knows God. 8 Whoever does not love does not know God, because God is love. 9 This is how God showed his love among us: He sent his one and only Son into the world that we might live through him. 10 This is love: not that we loved God, but that he loved us and sent his Son as an atoning sacrifice for our sins. 11 Dear friends, since God so loved us, we also ought to love one another. 12 No one has ever seen God; but if we love one another, God lives in us and his love is made complete in us.

13 This is how we know that we live in him and he in us: He has given us of his Spirit. 14 And we have seen and testify that the Father has sent his Son to be the Savior of the world. 15 If anyone acknowledges that Jesus is the Son of God, God lives in them and they in God. 16 And so we know and rely on the love God has for us.

God is love. Whoever lives in love lives in God, and God in them. 17 This is how love is made complete among us so that we will have confidence on the day of judgment: In this world we are like Jesus. 18 There is no fear in love. But perfect love drives out fear, because fear has to do with punishment. The one who fears is not made perfect in love.

19 We love because he first loved us. (1 John 4: 7-19)

PRAYER
"GOD, your amazing grace is truly amazing! Thank you for saving me. Thank you for loving me first. I love you, too! May my life be an ongoing reflection of your amazing grace and love. Amen."

Day 17
I Want to be Worthy

Teach the older men to exercise self-control, to be worthy of respect, and to live wisely. They must have sound faith and be filled with love and patience.
--Titus 2:2 (NLT)

What does it mean to be **worthy**?

Worthy: adj. Having worth, value, merit; honorable, or admirable.

Synonyms: *good, true, honest, honorable, reliable, trustworthy, dependable, noble, charitable, dutiful, philanthropic, virtuous, ethical, moral, pure, upright, righteous, decent, incorruptible, creditable, deserving, praiseworthy, right-minded, whole-souled, model, exemplary, sinless, blameless.*

We know that God is worthy to be praised! We know that God's character includes every word listed above, and much, much more than even our language can contain. He is worthy of it all!

*"I called to the Lord, **who is worthy of praise**, and have been saved from my enemies." (2 Samuel 22:4)*

*Great is the Lord and **most worthy of praise**; his greatness no one can fathom. Psalm (145:3)*

GOD is WORTHY! But, am I?

I'm a Christian. I'm supposed to be like Jesus. I am a follower and disciple of Jesus. When others look at me and my life, they should see Christ in me. *But do they?*

I want to be viewed by God as a worthy servant. I want to be viewed by God as a worthy friend who can be entrusted with God's best gifts, talents, treasure, relationships, wisdom, and His word.

God has made a **deposit** into each one of us. When each of us accepts Jesus as our Lord and Savior, many things happen in addition to salvation and the promise of eternal life: God places Himself into you and me. It's *amazing!*

Jesus Promises the Holy Spirit
*16 And I will ask the Father, and he will give you another advocate to help you and be with you forever— 17 the Spirit of truth. The world cannot accept him, because it neither sees him nor knows him. But you know him, **for he lives with you and will be in you.** 18 I will not leave you as orphans; I will come to you. (John 14:16-18)*

God makes his home in you and me.
23 Jesus replied, "Anyone who loves me will obey my teaching. My Father will love them, and we will come to them and make our home with them. (John 14:23)

A deposit of the Holy Spirit has been placed into our hearts. And that makes us worthy.

* * *

BE STRONG!

1. **God calls you and sees you as a worthy home for his Holy Spirit.**
   a. Can you accept that gift?
   b. Can you embrace it and live your life as a "living temple" of the most high God?

What are your thoughts?

2. **You are God's representative** in your home, office, work space, on the streets you drive, in stores that you shop, in the life that you live. Wherever you are, God is with you. You represent Him.
   How's that going?

What are your thoughts?

PRAYER

"God, you chose to make your home in me. That's crazy, that You'd select someone like me to move in with! Wow! I'm so honored and privileged to be worthy of your intimate presence. Thank you. I need help living as a man in whom You abide. Consume every thought and action that is not aligned with Your will for my life. Help me to get to know You more, so that I can reflect You in all that I do. Thank you, Jesus! Amen."

Day 18
Making a Deposit of Great Value

*Now it is God who makes both us and you stand firm in Christ. He anointed us, set his seal of ownership on us, and put **his Spirit in our hearts as a deposit**, guaranteeing what is to come.*
--2 Corinthians 1:21-22

Have you ever opened a savings account in a bank and invested some money? Sure, you have. You deposit something of value to you into the bank, you entrust it to them. One day, you'll be back to retrieve what you've saved there. It doesn't matter if the banker knows when you'll be back. The bank is entrusted to care for your money for all the time you entrust it to them. Because they have had the privilege of caring for your money for a period of time, when you come back unannounced, you expect the full value plus some interest on the deposit. The length of time that your money has been on deposit determines how much more money you get back. This is called a **Return On Investment,** or ROI.

Return on Investment (ROI) is a performance measure used to evaluate the efficiency of an investment or to compare the efficiency of a number of different investments.[20]

God has deposited Himself into you, and He expects a high return on his investment.

Have you ever thought of God seeing *you* as a worthy investment of Himself? Apparently, He sees you as someone worthy to receive His deposit of the Holy Spirit, a deposit of Himself. When you accepted Jesus as your Savior, several things changed forever!

The Parable of the Bags of Gold (or Talents)

20

https://www.investopedia.com/terms/r/returnoninvestment.asp

14 *"Again, it will be like a man going on a journey, who called his servants and entrusted his wealth to them. 15 To one he gave five bags of gold, to another two bags, and to another one bag, each according to his ability. Then he went on his journey. 16 The man who had received five bags of gold went at once and put his money to work and gained five bags more. 17 So also, the one with two bags of gold gained two more. 18 But the man who had received one bag went off, dug a hole in the ground and hid his master's money.*

19 *"After a long time the master of those servants returned and settled accounts with them. 20 The man who had received five bags of gold brought the other five. 'Master,' he said, 'you entrusted me with five bags of gold. See, I have gained five more.'*

21 *"His master replied, 'Well done, good and faithful servant! You have been faithful with a few things; I will put you in charge of many things. Come and share your master's happiness!'*

22 *"The man with two bags of gold also came. 'Master,' he said, 'you entrusted me with two bags of gold; see, I have gained two more.'*

23 *"His master replied, 'Well done, good and faithful servant! You have been faithful with a few things; I will put you in charge of many things. Come and share your master's happiness!'*

24 *"Then the man who had received one bag of gold came. 'Master,' he said, 'I knew that you are a hard man, harvesting where you have not sown and gathering where you have not scattered seed. 25 So I was afraid and went out and hid your gold in the ground. See, here is what belongs to you.'*

26 *"His master replied, 'You wicked, lazy servant! So you knew that I harvest where I have not sown and gather where I have not scattered seed? 27 Well then, you should have put my money on deposit with the bankers, so that when I returned I would have received it back with interest.*

28 *"'So take the bag of gold from him and give it to the one who has ten bags. 29 For whoever has will be given more, and they will have an abundance. Whoever does not have, even what they have will be taken from them. 30 And throw that worthless servant outside, into the darkness, where there will be weeping and gnashing of teeth.'*
(Matthew 25:14-30)

*   *   *

BE STRONG!

1. **God sees you as worthy to be "investment grade" quality**! What kind of return will you present to the Master when He asks?

What are your thoughts?

2. **Which servant do you best identify with in your life?**
   a. The servant with one bag
   b. The servant with four bags
   c. The servant with eleven bags

What are your thoughts?

NOTE: If you do not identify with the servant who received eleven bags, why not? What will it take for you to accept that it is possible to be the man who says, "Look, GOD has entrusted me with eleven!"

PRAYER

"God, your love is amazing, and You entrust so much of Yourself to us. May we grow into becoming the servants who are worthy of eleven bags. Amen!"

Be Strong!

Day 19
Spiritual Attacks are Real

"The thief comes only to steal and kill and destroy;
I have come that they may have life and have it to the full."
--John 10:10a

If you are a friend of Jesus, then His enemies are your enemies. You have a target on your back, and you are being hunted. As a matter of fact, how *amazing* it is to be known as a friend of the Most High God, the Lamb of God, the Messiah, the Almighty, I AM, The Way, the Truth and the Life (John 14:6)!

On the other hand, if you are *not* a friend of Jesus, then don't worry about finishing this devotional—you've got much bigger issues to deal with first.

Jesus said this about the Enemy – his name is Satan, liar, thief, murderer, demon or the devil.

"You belong to your father, the devil, and you want to carry out your father's desires. He was a murderer from the beginning, not holding to the truth, for there is no truth in him. When he lies, he speaks his native language, for he is a liar and the father of lies." (John 8:44)

"The thief comes only to steal and kill and destroy; I have come that they may have life and have it to the full." (John 10:10a)

Be alert and of sober mind. Your enemy the devil prowls around like a roaring lion looking for someone to devour. Resist him, standing firm in the faith, because you know that the family of believers throughout the world is undergoing the same kind of sufferings. (1 Peter 5:8-9)

What are we to do? We must "weapon up" for the spiritual battle!

Know who <u>YOU are</u>!

You, dear children, are from God and have overcome them,
because the one who is in you is greater than the one who is in the world.
John 4:4

7 Submit yourselves, then, to God. Resist the devil, and he will flee from
you. 8 Come near to God and he will come near to you...
James 4:7-8a

Know who <u>GOD is</u>!

Therefore God exalted him to the highest place
and gave him the name that is above every name,
that at the name of Jesus every knee should bow,
in heaven and on earth and under the earth,
and every tongue acknowledge that Jesus Christ is Lord,
to the glory of God the Father. (Philippians 2:9-11)

God loves all who hate evil, And those who love him he keeps safe,
Snatches them from the grip of the wicked. (Psalm 97:10) (MSG)

Put On the Armor of God

10 Finally, be strong in the Lord and in his mighty power. 11 Put on the full
armor of God, so that you can take your stand against the devil's schemes. 12
For our struggle is not against flesh and blood, but against the rulers, against
the authorities, against the powers of this dark world and against the spiritual
forces of evil in the heavenly realms. 13 Therefore put on the full armor of
God, so that when the day of evil comes, you may be able to stand your ground,
and after you have done everything, to stand. 14 Stand firm then, with the
belt of truth buckled around your waist, with the breastplate of righteousness
in place, 15 and with your feet fitted with the readiness that comes from the
gospel of peace. 16 In addition to all this, take up the shield of faith, with
which you can extinguish all the flaming arrows of the evil one. 17 Take the
helmet of salvation and the sword of the Spirit, which is the word of God.
18 And pray in the Spirit on all occasions with all kinds of prayers and
requests. With this in mind, be alert and always keep on praying for all the
Lord's people. (Ephesians 6: 10-18)

*   *   *

BE STRONG!

1. **Be STRONG! Get your strength from Jesus!** Not your own physical/mental/financial strength! No, you need *God's strength*—He will supply!
   a. Get in God's word and replace the enemy's lies with God's TRUTH!
   b. Memorize one or more of the scriptures above – it's your strength and life!

2. **Know your enemy**: he is not flesh & blood, and he will attack where you are most vulnerable (weak). If you do not know your weakness, you are extremely vulnerable to attack.
   a. Where are you weak (check your heart and thoughts)?
   b. Create a list of your weaknesses, brokenness, sinfulness, etc.

   <u>List your Top Three most vulnerable weaknesses.</u>
   1.
   2.
   3.

3. Lastly, you need to surround yourself with friends of Jesus. Men, who are the front lines of this spiritual battle? Other holy men. Do you have a group of men in your life? If not, get one! I suggest signing up for a *Marked Men for Christ* ministry *Phase 1* experience; you'll be surrounded by strong, holy men. To learn more and register, go to: www.markedmenforchrist.org

PRAYER

"Jesus, I am victorious because of YOU! You defeated death when you came out of that grave! Praise YOU, Bless YOU, Thank YOU, LORD! You call me friend. You know me. I want to stand in Your strength (not my strength). For with JESUS, I am STRONG! Amen!"

Day 20
Fear is a Choice

"Do not be afraid," Jesus said. --Mark 5:36

There are, of course, different types of fear. Let's focus on the type of fear that has these well-known synonyms; terror, panic, horror, despair, anxiety, worry, cowardice, fright, timidity, trepidation, etc.

Fear is a choice.

In Mark 5:36, Jesus offers us the choice: be afraid, or just believe. Fear is clearly one of the enemy's weapons to use against us. Have you ever considered that fear is a choice? I can choose to have anxiety and worry about a situation or I could choose a different path. I could choose to trust that GOD's got this. GOD is in control and no matter what happens, HE has a great plan for me – if, I simply choose to trust (believe) Him and do *His* will in this situation.

Choose to Not Have Fear:

1. "for God gave us a spirit not of fear but of power and love and self-control." (2 Timothy 1:7) (ESV)
2. "For I, the Lord your God, hold your right hand; it is I who say to you, "Fear not, I am the one who helps you." Fear not, you worm Jacob, you men of Israel! I am the one who helps you, declares the Lord; your Redeemer is the Holy One of Israel." (Isaiah 41:13-14) (ESV)
3. "So do not fear, for I am with you; do not be dismayed, for I am your God. I will strengthen you and help you; I will uphold you with my righteous right hand." (Isaiah 41:10)
4. "When I am afraid, I put my trust in you." (Psalm 56:3)
5. "Do not be anxious about anything, but in every situation, by prayer and petition, with thanksgiving, present your requests to God. And the peace of God, which transcends

all understanding, will guard your hearts and your minds in Christ Jesus." (Philippians 4:6-7)

6. "Peace I leave with you; my peace I give you. I do not give to you as the world gives. Do not let your hearts be troubled and do not be afraid." (John 14:27)

7. "There is no fear in love. But perfect love drives out fear, because fear has to do with punishment. The one who fears is not made perfect in love." (1 John 4:18)

8. "Even though I walk through the valley of the shadow of death, I will fear no evil, for you are with me; your rod and your staff, they comfort me." (Psalm 23:4) (ESV)

9. "Have I not commanded you? Be strong and courageous. Do not be frightened, and do not be dismayed, for the Lord your God is with you wherever you go.." (Joshua 1:9) (ESV)

10. "Therefore do not worry about tomorrow, for tomorrow will worry about itself. Each day has enough trouble of its own." (Matthew 6:34)

11. "Then Jesus said to his disciples: "Therefore I tell you, do not worry about your life, what you will eat; or about your body, what you will wear. 23 For life is more than food, and the body more than clothes. 24 Consider the ravens: They do not sow or reap, they have no storeroom or barn; yet God feeds them. And how much more valuable you are than birds! 25 Who of you by worrying can add a single hour to your life[a]? 26 Since you cannot do this very little thing, why do you worry about the rest?" (Luke 12:22-26)

12. "The Lord is my light and my salvation—whom shall I fear? The Lord is the stronghold of my life—of whom shall I be afraid?" (Psalm 27:1) (ESV)

* * *

BE STRONG!

1. Check yourself – do you tend to choose *fear* more than *trust* (faith)? YES/NO
2. Look backward over your life – can you see a pattern of how you have done this over and over?
3. Now look forward – can you decide today to change the pattern of your life by choosing to *TRUST GOD* (faith in God)? YES/NO
4. As you go forward, find your trust in God by building your faith in God through His words of life (scripture). Will you commit to turning to God's Word the next time you feel fear?

PRAYER

"Jesus – you are my ROCK, my firm FOUNDATION of which I can stand. I do trust you, Lord. Help me grow in my faith and trust in YOU. Help me to not fall into my fears, but instead fall into your loving caring arms as you carry me though my struggles. Thank you, JESUS! Amen!"

Day 21
MUST LOVE

*"A new command I give you: Love one another. As I have loved
you, so you **must** love one another."*
--John 13:34-35

After spending several years with His disciples, Jesus is preparing
to depart from them, and He says that he has a *NEW
COMMANDMENT.*

Perhaps his disciples were thinking, "What? Why did you wait
so long to give it to us?" But Jesus did not wait too long; His
timing is always perfect!

These "students" needed to graduate from the multi-year
training, and during these final hours of Jesus' life on earth, He
told them these words

JOHN 13:34 (4 Translations of this passage): "must LOVE"

New International Version
"A new command I give you: Love one another. As I have
loved you, so you **must** love one another.

New Living Translation (NLT)
So now I am giving you a new commandment: Love each
other. Just as I have loved you, you **should** love each
other.

English Standard Version (ESV)
A new commandment I give to you, that you love one
another: just as I have loved you, you also **are to** love one
another.

King James Bible (KJV)
A new commandment I give unto you, That ye love one
another; as I have loved you, that ye **also** love one
another.

Did you notice the word "LOVE" in this one verse? Question: How many times did Jesus use that word? Read each translation again. Look up additional translations and see how many times Jesus says; "love."
ANSWER: 3

A NEW commandment in one verse that uses the SAME WORD 3-times. Jesus is making his key point (my paraphrase): "For the entire time that you have spent with me, I have modeled or demonstrated **love** to you and to **everyone** that we have encountered together. **I Am Love,** and you are to do what I have shown you (modeled for you). And the result of you loving everyone will result in you being known in the world as my disciples."

JOHN 13:35 (4 Translations of this passage): "they will KNOW"

New International Version
By this everyone will <u>know</u> that you are my disciples, if you love one another."

New Living Translation (NLT)
Your love for one another will <u>prove</u> to the world that you are my disciples."

English Standard Version (ESV)
By this all people will <u>know</u> that you are my disciples, if you have love for one another.

King James Bible (KJV)
By this shall all men <u>know</u> that ye are my disciples, if ye have love one to another.

* * *

BE STRONG!

1. To be a disciple of Jesus, your life "MUST" reflect God's love for others. Now, it is easy to love those who are lovable – right? Make a list of the _easy-to-love_ people in your life.

2. To be a disciple of Jesus, your life "MUST" reflect God's love for others. Is it easy to love those who are not lovable? Make a list of the <u>not</u>-easy-to-love people in your life.

3. Think about this: looking back over your life, reflect on the good days and not- so-good days of your existence on the planet. Now ask yourself this question; Which list would Jesus put your name on? The easy-to-love list? Or not-easy-to-love?

PRAYER

"Jesus, forgive me for the many days that I have called myself a Christian (disciple of Yours) and have <u>not</u> modeled Your love. Instead, I have been selfish, self-centered, arrogant, prideful, self-consuming, etc. Forgive me, Lord. I want to be like YOU. Help me to love others as you have loved. Amen!"

About the Author

Steve "Spice" Spicer married his Texas high school sweetheart, Debi. The week of their wedding began with a whirlwind: he graduated from Rice University on Friday; they got married three days later on Monday; they relocated from central Texas to New Orleans on Tuesday; and Spice started his professional career on Wednesday. Their life transitions didn't allow for a honeymoon then, so they've honeymooned for each of their thirty-seven years.

Spice invested decades as a corporate leader with Procter and Gamble, and together, with help from countless others, they have launched two international ministries: *Marked Men for Christ* and *Women's Walk with Christ*. Spice and Debi live in Colorado near their two sons, Zach (married to Katy) and Scott.

Spice's life mission: As a *Marked Man for Christ*, I co-create a loving world by modeling the love of Jesus Christ; with great faith, wisdom and holiness.

About *Marked Men for Christ* Ministries

Marked Men for Christ **ministry has one purpose: To build STRONGER men for JESUS CHRIST** (from the inside-out). We do this as a partner to the church men's ministry.

HOW

We create a safe environment. It is an Intense-Masculine-Powerful 44-hour experience! We invite men to go deep into their heart and seek the healing of their brokenness through the power of the Holy Spirit. We DO what God's word says in James 5:16! Thousands of men are now living their God-given life mission; at home, work, church, etc.

Look deep within themselves at 5-potentially wounded/broken areas of their life; Deceit, Fear, Anger, Sadness and Shame – seeking God's healing. This happens in the first 24-hours. Then, the next 20-hours, we focus on celebrating and honoring GOD for what HE has done! Discovering God's entrusted talents, gifts and blessings, every man will know his life's purpose (mission) before they leave. After the 44-hour experience -- we encourage men to go back to their local church! Share with your pastor what you discovered about yourself!

There is MORE! Phase 2 are our weekly follow-up sessions (2-hours/week) in small groups! The "Christian faith strength training continues for God's men..."

Be Strong!

RESULTS

In 18-years; over 11,000 men, on 4-continents from over 2,200 churches across 30-countries have experienced the life transforming healing power of our Lord Jesus Christ through *Marked Men for Christ* ministry! Pray about attending. **www.markedmenforchrist.org**

OUR MISSION: As a Holy Spirit led global ministry, we build **STRONGER MEN for JESUS CHRIST** through ongoing transformative experiences and authentic relationships.

OUR VISION: MEN throughout the world being healed and made whole and living in mission through the power of JESUS CHRIST for HIS CHURCH.

Contact *Marked Men for Christ* ministry:

Website: www.markedmenforchrist.org

Questions: info@markedmenforchrist.org

Women's ministry: www.womenswalkwithchrist.org